Once U~~pon~~

Growing Up in the 1950s

-Michael Bourgo-

-2019-

Author Photograph: Jennie Bourgo

Independently published by the author

Some of the poems in this book are reprinted from *Moments Past and Present* (2016) and *More Moments* (2017)

To the memory of our parents:

Nelle Coggins Bourgo (1905-1983)

Alfred Bartlett Bourgo (1915-1979)

Contents

A Prologue

My brother and I are the sons of Alfred Bartlett Bourgo and Nelle Coggins Bourgo. Al and Nelle came from very different settings and heritages, though one thing they had in common was a modest background. Neither had a distinguished ancestry and both benefited from the efforts of a father who managed to find a path upwards. As far as we know they were the first in their families to attend college, though our mother never quite managed to graduate. They may have also been the first to finish high school.

Our father was born in Joliet, Illinois, in 1915. His ancestry consisted mostly of recent immigrants from Ireland, Quebec, and Germany, though one of his grandfathers was a classic Anglo-Saxon Protestant whose forebears had settled in colonial Massachusetts. By the time Alfred Bartlett came along, the Bourgos had managed to climb into the middle class. His father rose to be the Assistant Postmaster of Joliet, which provided security, especially during the Depression years and allowed Dad to finish his college degree in civil engineering in 1937.

He had a problematic relationship with his family. At the age of eight, his mother died, and though he never talked about her, it was understandably a difficult and emotional event. His father wasted little time pursuing another spouse and was soon courting a widow named Jenny Carlson who worked at a local bank. She came from a large family of Carlsons who lived in the Joliet area. As was often the case with recent immigrants, the tribe had not made a full transition to their new country. Many of them still preferred to speak Swedish, observed holidays and habits from the old country and served up Swedish fare at their gatherings.

It would be easy to characterize Jenny as the evil stepmother. She did make every effort to eliminate the ties with her predecessor's family. Dad had spent a lot of time with his mother's relatives in Morris, a town some twenty miles west of Joliet. All that came to an end under the new regime. Instead, the family connections tilted to the Carlsons. Our father once mentioned off hand that he might have liked some of them if he could have understood their conversations. In any event, he disliked Jenny and her efforts to dote on him only made matters worse.

He also came to have reservations about his father, both for subjecting him to Jenny and for his relentless efforts to conform to the norms of small-town respectability. Alfred the elder was an inveterate joiner of clubs, fraternities and so forth. He modeled his life after George Bartlett, his first father-in-law. George was the sort of man who could have served as a model for Babbitt—a realtor with a generous dose of boosterism. Though I think some of our

Alfred Meagher and Alfred Bartlett, 1938

father's disapproval was mitigated by gratitude for the opportunities his father gave him, he was a lifelong non-joiner and lost almost all connection with his family. The only member of his family we ever got to know was one aunt.

Mother was born in Knoxville, Tennessee, in 1905. Her father, Elbert Coggins, grew up in dire rural poverty. His father, Jesse, was a Confederate veteran and likely illiterate. A hardworking man who had hard luck all his life, he was a farmer who never managed to own a farm and rarely held a job for any length of time. Life was grim in Tennessee after the Civil War, and Elbert managed only a few years of formal education. He went to work in his teens for the Southern Railroad and stayed with the company for 52 years. A ferocious learner, he taught himself to read (his favorite authors were God, Charles Dickens, Robert W. Service, and Elbert Hubbard) and mastered the science of laying track. Over time, he was promoted to the rank of district track supervisor. Aside from his job and his family, fishing and the Quaker church were at the center of his life.

Her mother, Grace Thomas Coggins, was from more genteel circumstances. Her origins were Quaker and her father was a store owner in a small town northeast of Knoxville called Friends Station. She was thirteen years younger than her husband, and his second wife (the first having passed away). At age 19 she inherited an eight-year-old stepson and within a few short years, she had two more of her own to take care of. In time Grace and Elbert had seven children separated over twenty years, but two died in infancy. In addition Grace, like all three of her daughters, had difficult pregnancies and suffered at least three miscarriages.

Such a large family, widely spread by ages, led to occasional tension among the siblings, especially in adulthood. Still, all Grace's children stayed in contact with each other throughout their lives (though only our mother and her brother Kelsey had a relationship with their half-brother, Neil), even as they scattered across the country after 1945. My brother and I thus had no shortage of aunts and uncles, or for that matter, cousins. Though the cousins have not all stayed in touch with each other, my brother and I have had lifelong relationships with several of them. Unlike the Bourgo side

9

of things, we saw members of the Coggins tribe on a pretty regular basis.

The 1918-1919 flu pandemic did not claim any lives among the Coggins, but Grace was hit very hard. Her heart was badly damaged and she was bedridden for many months. Although she finally recovered, she was a semi-invalid for the rest of her life (somehow managing to have two additional daughters in 1922 and 1925). Nelle, the oldest girl, filled in as substitute mother in 1919 (missing an entire year of school) and thereafter intermittently when Grace was not well. My Aunt Betty (born in 1925) always said Nelle was her real mother. Such extensive duties at home did not help our mother's prospects for marriage, and by her late 20s, she was prepared to be an old maid.

After graduating from the University of Illinois in 1937, our father accepted a position with the newly formed Tennessee Valley Authority and began a forty-year career in hydraulics—dams, flood control, irrigation, and electrical generation. This necessitated

Our mother around the time that she got married—1940 or 1941

relocating to Knoxville where TVA headquarters were situated and given his modest salary ($175 per month), he decided to live at the YMCA.

Over the years Nelle had a series of jobs, but having majored in home economics at college, she inclined to food service as a career. She had a bruising experience at the local Woolworth's, where, as the manager of the lunch counter, she had to deal with a very contentious boss. This soured her on working for other people. Eventually, she left Woolworth's and struck out on her own, acquiring the franchise for the lunch room at the YMCA.

I suspect the rest of the story can be left to your imagination.

The First Miracle

In a life full of miracles,
you can't overlook the very first one,
and so today I am wondering
why our parents met,
what in all the universe
pulled them into that meeting
and how they decided,
those two unlikely people,
to have another and another,
until meetings were replaced
by the union of their every days.

He was that apprentice engineer
who took the job at the TVA,
and moved far away from home,
probably the first time in his 22 years
he'd ever crossed the borders of Illinois,
but confident of his desire to marry;

and she, that stubborn woman
determined to earn her own way,
disillusioned with earlier romance,
with ambitions to be an old maid,
but who managed the dining room
at the YMCA where he lived;

and at the end of this tale,
our father was hard to discourage:
in this, as throughout his life
a decision was no small thing.
His persistence was formidable—
as was hers—until one certain day,
she decided for both of them,
and let him change her mind.

1720 Lombard Street (1949)

It was a home built for a hero
back from France or the Pacific,
a modest house on a narrow lot,
four tiny rooms perched on a slab
in a long row of white cracker boxes
lined up on both sides of the street,
differing only in the color of their shutters.

 Behind the house was dusty clay,
broken ground that grew only weeds,
where careless and hurried builders
had pitched their debris into the field,
turning small boys into archeologists,
uncovering lush and useful treasures
of wire, pipes, and lumber.

As we wandered through the summer
Dickie, George and I acquired a leader.
Henry was several years older,
a designer with skill and imagination,
who could transform our findings
into a range of forts and castles
aimed at fierce but unnamed enemies.

 On warm and humid evenings,
in that precious time between dinner and bed,
the adults would gather in front yards,
circles of lawn chairs and laughter,
while we darted like minnows
through the shadows between the houses,
hoping that one of them would hear
the bell on the ice cream truck.

1720 Lombard Street in 1949: Mother with her two savages. Center is
Emily Newbill, a neighbor, and right, our mother's sister Betty Bustin.
Emily is holding Betty's little girl, our cousin Tenna. The hutch resides in
my home today along with the Modern Library edition volumes on the
shelves to the lower left. The needlepoint picture above the books hangs in
my brother's home.

The Early Years in Knoxville

I was born on November 19, 1944, in Knoxville, Tennessee. Our father had been shipped out to Europe along with the rest of the 41st Engineering Regiment in the spring of that year, and our mother had her hands full. In addition to being pregnant (at age 39), she had two invalid parents to look after, a younger sister just out of high school, and I suspect she had not yet finished mourning the loss of her first child, a daughter who was stillborn in April 1943. She talked about that girl off and on for the rest of her life.

Like her father, Nelle was resourceful, self-sufficient and utterly disinclined to self-pity. Whatever the challenge, she always managed to meet it head on, and this time must have been no different. I was duly ushered into the world and finally met my father early in 1946. The 41st reflected the old order in the United States. It was a segregated army that won the war and all the enlisted personnel in our father's unit were African Americans, while most of the officers were white. As such, the 41st was relegated to the end of the line and had to wait almost a year after VE-Day to get a ride home. My meeting with Captain Al Bourgo was classically inauspicious. I was a wary toddler and family tradition relates I started howling when he picked me up for the first time.

For the first year or so we all lived on Oklahoma Avenue in the family home. My grandmother had died in 1945 and my grandfather passed away in early 1947. After his death, Al and Nelle took advantage of the VA loan program and purchased a four-room house at 1720 Lombard Street in Knoxville. Lombard was a short street (two blocks or so) and lined with houses almost identical to ours. It was a modest home in the truest sense of the word. Laid out on a concrete slab were two bedrooms, a living room, and a kitchen with a dining area.

My first memories (perhaps about age 3) are from this home. I soon had two pals to play with, George Kreisel and Dickie Sharp. We enjoyed our play together, but Dickie was sometimes rambunctious and whacked me in the head one day with a board, leaving a scar on my forehead that is visible to this day. George was a milder sort of fellow and a visit to his home was always a treat, as his mother stocked an endless supply of tasty snacks. However, Mrs. Kreisel did not pass out the goodies. That job was left to their black housekeeper—Knoxville was indeed in the South.

Mike and Al, spring 1946, at 345 East Oklahoma Avenue

Nothing we did was quite as much fun as following Henry Newbill around. Henry was six or seven and a one-man construction outfit. The builders of our homes had left all sorts of scrap in what passed for the backyard of our block of houses. There had been some effort to grow grass in the front but behind, it was never more than a weedy stretch of waste ground, but a paradise for small boys. Using the various boards, pipe and other material left behind, Henry constructed various and sundry buildings for us to play in, though he never managed to put a roof over our heads until he talked his mother out of an old sheet.

Henry's mother and mine had known each other in the past. Emily Newbill worked as a nurse and occasionally asked our mother to watch Henry. At other times Mrs. Newbill looked after me when Nelle had some errand she preferred to do without my assistance. Henry was not a successful student and at one point was struggling with reading. Our mother was enlisted to tutor Henry when he was with us and I attended the lessons. As she and Henry rehearsed the alphabet and the pronunciation for each letter, I started absorbing the material and before long one of my favorite things to do was to read the letters aloud from things like boxes of laundry soap ("O-x-y-d-o-l!"), canned foods and before long, the newspaper. I can still hear Mother telling Dad I was learning faster than poor Henry.

I am wary of these early memories. As time goes on, I wonder how much I recall from my own experience versus what someone told me later. Memories are fleeting stuff and often a series of images rather than the specific events of a particular day from one end to the other. So, without other details, I still remember leaving the doctor's office after just having lost my tonsils, the man across street setting fire to the webs of tent caterpillars, and the drama one night when a tanker truck caught fire on Riverside Drive about a half block from our home. It was one of the few times I ever witnessed fear in our mother. For a while, there was some concern the firemen might not be able to contain the spread of the blaze.

I have been an unadventurous type most of my life and have always been leery of breaking the rules. On several occasions, though, I managed to give Mother a scare. On one fine morning, I decided to take off down the street with some vague idea of exploration. Accompanied by our Scottish terrier, Keynote, I walked to Riverside Drive turned left, walked a block, turned left again and walked up Crestview Street (which ran parallel to Lombard). Before long some woman spotted me and realized I was on the loose. She took me into her home, and before long Mother showed up to collect me. The woman had not yet managed to identify who I was and where I lived, but she left old Key on her front stoop, which was the giveaway when Nelle's searches brought her up Crestview.

The other occasion was at Miller's department store when I managed to get on the escalator (which I loved) and took myself up to the second floor. My freedom was short lived and the discussion that ensued was not agreeable. Strangely enough, I don't remember any unpleasant words after running away with the dog. Perhaps our mother felt the same way I did as a parent when faced with similar circumstance: too grateful and too relieved to get mad at the kid.

I have clear memories of segregation. Knoxville was not deep South (in fact it had been pro-Union in the Civil War) but strict separation of the races was the norm. When we boarded the bus on Riverside Drive to go downtown, I wondered why the black people were standing in back when there were empty seats in the front area. The downtown department stores had water fountains in pairs, and Mother once had to grab me before I drank from the one labeled "colored." As she disagreed heartily with segregation, that water wouldn't have troubled her in the least, but she preferred to be discreet regarding the local customs.

I was about three and a half when my brother, Jon Meagher Bourgo, arrived on March 15, 1948. I can still picture being at home with Dad, sitting on a kitchen counter, and watching him heat something (no doubt from a can) for me to eat. I also have a faint recollection of Jon's arrival at the house, but few memories of him until he was a toddler. It did seem like a lot more effort to go downtown by bus once he arrived. His stroller had to be folded up and passed to the driver before we could all climb in.

Concurrent with the birth of Jon, some large changes were in store for all of us. After the war, our father returned briefly to the TVA, but then joined the Knoxville branch of a private firm, Frederick R. Harris, which was based in New York City. After a short tenure there he learned in early 1948 that the firm was going to close the Knoxville office. To stay with Harris he would have to apply for a position in one of their other offices. Al had never been happy at Harris and at age 32, he was eager to find a stable position where he could move up professionally. By happy coincidence, his mentor from TVA days, Calvin Davis, offered him a position in a small firm in Chicago, Harza Engineering, and Dad decided to take a chance. However, he and Nelle decided the family would remain behind for the time being until things were a little more assured. It was a separation that ended up lasting three years.

Father and sons, shortly before he left for Chicago in 1948.

As in the war years, our mother was on her own once more. We continued to live in the Lombard house until late 1949 or early 1950. At that point, in anticipation of an imminent move to Chicago, the house was sold and we moved to temporary (at least that was the plan) quarters at 323 East Hill Avenue.

We had a first-floor apartment in an old house that had been subdivided into flats. The neighborhood was grubby but within walking distance of downtown, where we occasionally ate at the S&W or Brown's, both venerable cafeterias that offered cornucopias of delights and friendly waiters who carried your tray to the table. About this time I went to the first movie I can recall. It was Disney's version of *The Legend of Sleepy Hollow*, and the scenes with the headless horseman scared the living daylights out of me.

Our stay at East Hill stretched to over a year, much longer than anticipated. It was not always as much fun as Lombard Street—

there were no other children to play with—though it was exciting to be downtown more often. It was also an early introduction to the varieties of urban life. Though I am sure Mother was assiduous in trying to shield us from some of the unsavory qualities of life on East Hill Street, she was not uniformly successful in that regard. Though the neighborhood was likely not a hotbed of crime, the police were regularly around.

Mike and Jon at 323 East Hill Street, 1950

I certainly missed our father. His visits were infrequent but welcome and we all tried our best to show him how much we appreciated having him home. One Christmas I demonstrated I could read and his response made me beam with pride. On one of these infrequent trips back to Knoxville, he came by plane, which made quite an impression on me. After seeing a Constellation airliner at the airport, I proceeded to build several planes in the back yard using orange crates and scrap wood. It was very convenient; as the crates had two compartments—a seat for me and one for Jon.

One of my backyard airplanes. From the look on my face, there must be some design flaw I haven't figured out yet.

In the fall of 1950 I was almost six, but not enrolled in school. There was no public kindergarten in Tennessee and Nelle had assumed my November birthday would make me ineligible to attend first grade. About five weeks into the term, she made a few inquiries and learned I would be allowed to start school. So off we went to the Bell House School for a meeting with the principal, Miss Jessup. I found her intimidating, but I passed muster and began my formal education under the tutelage of Miss Delia Roberts, who presided over the first grade.

Miss Roberts had a daunting set of responsibilities. She had over thirty children in the class and a wide range of ages to deal with. In those days, Tennessee did not require children to start school until age eight and some parents saw no reason to rush matters along. Consequently, I had classmates who were much older than I. It

21

became clear to me not everyone thought that school was important. I did, however, and thanks to our mother's tutoring at home, I was more than ready to tackle the challenges of being a first grader and always eager to provide the answer to Miss Roberts's queries. It is entirely possible I was too anxious to please and a bit of a prig.

With my cousins, Larry (left) and Allen (right) in Oak Ridge, Tennessee, probably in the summer of 1949. Yes, I am the guy wearing the beanie.

Bell House School was just a short walk from our apartment. Mother and Jon took me to school each morning and collected me in the afternoon. The school did not discharge students for lunch. Thus, I became the owner of a Hopalong Cassidy lunchbox that included a small thermos decorated with Hoppy's horse, Topper. I was inordinately proud of this possession, which was carefully packed every morning by our mother. Most of the kids had to settle for paper bags, so I felt very special. I was by no means unique in liking this product. In 1950 Aladdin Industries sales jumped exponentially thanks to the Hoppy lunchbox.

However, my days at Bell House were numbered and our lives as Southerners were ending. Over the winter of 1950-1951, our parents decided the future lay in Chicago. Dad was feeling secure at Harza and there was no further need to wait. Though I imagine I must have been excited, but I have no memory of how I reacted to this news. I suppose I had always assumed this would happen, and it was business as usual.

Finding the Dog (1949)

One fine October afternoon in Knoxville,
our middle-aged Scottie took his leave.
Our mother had no love for this animal,
but to disappoint a then-absent husband
was not an admissible option,
and we passed the rest of the day
searching and calling in vain.

It was a very quiet suppertime
until someone called with news of our dog,
and herding us into coats and hats,
our mother led us on a long bus ride,
starts and stops through a darkening city,
descending at last in a distant neighborhood
a few steps from a small frame house.

She knocked, and as the door opened,
we found a black woman watching us,
old Key at her feet wagging his tail,
and after some polite conversation,
the shared knowledge of women everywhere,
smiles, thanks, and a dollar were passed,
and the dog emerged, not a bit contrite.

With the customary expertise of a parent,
she quickly conjured a taxi,
negotiating a ride with the black cabby,
the two agreeing to overlook local customs.
Making a warm pile in the back seat,
mother, two small boys, and dog
were all delivered safely home,
along with questions for a lifetime.

323 East Hill Street (1950-51)

Once a fine home near downtown,
it had become four seedy apartments,
a place our mother reluctantly moved us,
her plans for the briefest of transitions
turning into a long and trying year.
Oblivious to our parents' dilemma,
I plunged into months of excitement.

Across the hall was Mrs. Osborne,
nostalgic for Newark, New Jersey,
for whom I provided a willing audience.
Upstairs were the Misses Jenkins and Kenney,
a grandmotherly sort who gave us cookies
and a somewhat younger blond,
who entertained her friends.

I could scarcely believe our good fortune:
we could walk downtown to the movies,
someone left orange crates in the alley
that I turned into airplanes,
and one of Miss Kenney's admirers
fired his pistol into the backyard,
bringing a crowd and two policemen.

That fall, Miss Jenkins departed on a stretcher
and Miss Kenney by means unknown.
I started first grade at Bell House School,
the proud owner of a new lunch box,
and the champion speller in the class.
On the last day, as we were departing,
the kitchen ceiling abruptly collapsed.
Mother closed the door and we left.

Moving to Aurora (1951)

Moving north to rejoin our father was Mother's most ardent wish. For three long years, she had to run the show on her own in Knoxville, and I am sure it was often not a cheerful situation. I have never been certain why they waited three years before getting the three Tennesseans moved to the Chicago area. Over the years various reasons popped up. I was told the post-war housing shortage made it difficult to find a place to live in the sort of community they thought appropriate. Although both our parents appreciated Chicago, they thought it would be a mistake to live in the city. Dad had grown up in Joliet, and Aurora was similar but with a far better commuter rail link.

Another set of reasons had to do with the work situation. Dad knew he was taking a chance with Harza Engineering. While the owner was a noted civil engineer, his firm consisted of fewer than ten employees when our father joined in 1948. For a while, the firm lived from project to project, but soon enough, available money for infrastructure began to grow in the post-war years, both domestically and overseas. Before long Harza had a reasonable backlog of work and enough people to begin taking on multiple projects. While the firm always had work in the US, the overseas projects rapidly became the firm's largest revenue contributor, and our father's role was almost exclusively in the international division.

Mother also once told me, somewhat offhand, that she had felt her husband should have a few years to get his career launched without the distractions of home and family. Thanks to the war and the Depression, he was getting a late start in what would be his life's work and led to a very successful career (eventually he became CEO of Harza). I gathered this did not explain the initial separation but may have had something to do with it growing to three years. In addition, his frequent travels overseas (he was active in Central America at this point) were certainly a factor.

In the early months of 1951 things began to happen. First, we traveled up to Chicago to begin the house hunting process in late winter. We stayed in the Aurora Hotel in downtown Aurora, which my brother and I found to be both entertaining and novel. We enjoyed the coffee shop in the hotel because we could sit on a banquette along a window with a great view of a dam on the Fox River. From time to time a piece of driftwood would get hung up behind the dam, and we would watch it several times a day until it got free and resumed its journey downstream. I remember only a few details of our first stay in Aurora. It was cold outside, and our parents kept crackers and Kraft pimento cheese in the room. To this day, the taste of that concoction takes me back.

We looked at several apartments during this process. The search was complicated by the two of us and Keynote, our Scottish terrier. Finding a place that would accept children and a dog involved a lengthy effort. My only memories are of the place we did take—three rooms in a once gracious 19th-century house at 413 Downer Place that had been remodeled into apartments. There were five units—one in the basement, occupied by the owner's son (who acted as the super), two on the first floor, and two on the second floor. Our home was on the second floor. The flat across the hall was occupied by the Coleson family and it was the deluxe unit, including a portion of the second floor and the entire third floor.

So before long, we were back in Knoxville. It was a brief final sojourn before we were on the train again and headed back to Chicago. The movers had come, packed us up and I had said goodbye to my first-grade teacher, Miss Roberts. I had become quite attached to her and was a bit wistful when we left Bell House School the final time.

I have always wondered how Nelle felt about leaving Knoxville. She was 46 years old and had never lived anywhere else (other than a few short stints in North Carolina while Dad was in the army). However, she was widely traveled and as I would observe, time after time, an eminently competent and adaptable soul. Plus, I am sure she was thrilled to be back with her husband. Their obvious lifelong affection for each other was a gift to their sons whose value cannot be underestimated.

The second train ride north was quite intriguing since we had a traveling companion, our pal Keynote. I was both pleased and puzzled. I wasn't sure dogs were welcome on trains (they certainly were forbidden on buses), but our mother assured us all was just fine. Our porter greeted old Key warmly and relieved us of walking duties at several stops. Keynote took it all in stride, though I do wonder how we managed to get the dog from Chicago out to Aurora. I am not sure dogs were quite as welcome in the open coaches of the Burlington commuter trains as they were in Pullman compartments. Once in Aurora, my recollection is that he was not with us in the hotel, so I suppose he was exiled to a kennel.

We were once again at the Aurora Hotel, while we waited for the mover to show up. It felt like forever, but I expect it was no more than a week. The great day finally came and we moved into our new home. The weather was much warmer (it was now early April) and Jon and I were turned outside to explore a large and promising yard. Before long we were riding our tricycles up and down the sidewalk on Downer Place. By contrast with the sidewalks I knew in Knoxville they seemed very level and smooth.

Certain features of life in Aurora were novel. Garbage pickup was strictly limited to disposal of small amounts of "wet" garbage (which had to be wrapped in newspaper) and other non-combustibles such as glass and cans. "Dry garbage" was to be burned in an incinerator, which Jon and I thought to be a fine way to handle matters. I yearned for the day when I would be considered old enough to strike a match and start a conflagration. Air quality in Aurora must have been compromised by all that burning trash, particularly in the fall when people also burned leaves.

Behind the house and along an alley was a long garage with six separate stalls. Each apartment was allocated one spot and the sixth was rented to some man whom I do not recall, but I can still see what he was storing in his garage: iron lungs, a well-known piece of medical technology during the years when polio outbreaks were common every summer. It was rather ominous to look at these devices and then to think of that photo seen in *Life* of someone entirely enclosed in the apparatus save for the head.

Leading down from our back porch (just off the kitchen) was a long, steep open staircase that always troubled our mother. We were only permitted on those stairs if she was with us; normally we used the front stairs, which were inside the building. Sure enough, her fears were realized one day when my brother's hand slipped out of hers and he tumbled down the entire length. For once in her life, Nelle confessed, she absolutely froze. Mary Coleson was nearby hanging out clothes to dry and immediately went into action. She raced over to the stairs and virtually caught Jon on the bounce as he came off the last step. There was a doctor's office across the street and Mary had him over there in no time, our mother trailing behind and fearing the worst. Fortunately, he was a sturdy (and lucky) little fellow and suffered no apparent harm, but it became one of those moments of parental guilt that never leave our memories.

Our other parent was now once again part of our day-to-day life after three long years during which we might see him briefly just a few times each year. Since he had left when my brother was six weeks old, Jon did not know him at all. I had memories, but for all practical purposes, I was starting from close to zero, too. I can well recall I was nervous around him at first, but our father (who could disarm just about anyone) had little trouble convincing me there was nothing to fear. Very soon we would be sitting on the front steps every evening just before dinner time, waiting for him to step off the Downer-Western bus.

Not long after we moved into the new quarters, our mother set about getting me back into first grade. We walked over to Mary A. Todd Elementary, where the school administration got off to a poor start with Mother. Aurora had experienced numerous recent migrants from the South and the general conclusion was that students from that region were ill-prepared for learning. The principal (not the sainted Charles Friday of my later school years, but his predecessor) did a poor job of concealing his disdain for Southerners, their IQ's and their occasional lack of footwear.

I have always suspected the remarks about shoes set her indignation off as much as anything. True enough, in her girlhood, many Southern children went barefoot for much of the year, but her father made it a point of pride that his children always had a pair of shoes. In the South, in the early 20th century, having shoes on all one's children was solid evidence of industry and respectability. As it became apparent over the years that I was one of the better students in my class, our mother always found sweet revenge in recounting her tale of the uncharitable reception we got the first day.

Mike and Jon in front of 413 Downer Place, about 1953.

Whatever the principal's doubts, I was admitted to first grade and placed under the tutelage of Miss Lane. Miss Lane, likewise, was dubious about my abilities at the beginning but she quickly changed her mind when she discovered I could already read and write (thanks to Mother's tutoring) at a higher level than most of the other children. The one difficulty I recall from my early days at Mary A. Todd was that I did not know how to tie my shoes. This was a serious problem at the point in the day when we all changed to our sneakers for recess. Fortunately, I managed to find a friend who was willing to overlook this shortcoming and give me a hand. Her name was Lorraine McDonald and she willingly tied my shoes twice a day, though she did observe it was a skill one was expected to learn in kindergarten. I don't remember if I had the courage to tell her I had not been able to attend kindergarten in Tennessee. I was already self-conscious enough since I was regularly reminded I had a strange way of talking.

As things turned out, though, I was not to spend a great deal of time in Miss Lane's class that spring. We had only been in our new home a few weeks before the Coleson girls next door came down with the measles. Soon Jon and I joined them on the sick list. In those days measles was an automatic two-week quarantine. At just about the point we were officially over the measles, we both came down with chickenpox, once again thanks to Libby and her sister. The whole process was repeated once again, meaning I missed the better part of four weeks of school. I can recall feeling quite ill with the measles, but the chicken pox was just an annoyance. By the end of our second quarantine, we must have been a handful. We were both anxious to resume life and go outside. There's nothing worse than standing at a window watching other kids having a good time.

After all these medical calamities I attended less than 6 weeks of first grade in Aurora. Nelle and Al were both concerned the school would make me repeat first grade, but in the end, all was well. I was duly promoted to second grade and moved up another notch in my progress towards becoming a civilized being.

The Fox River

A river is almost a sacrament,
a mystery of origins and destinations,
from headwaters to mouth the span of a sea,
its channel a course through imagination
that collects the colors and stories
of everything along its banks,
and floats them off to far places.

Granted, this is not much of a river.
A stream once graced by the canoes
of the nation that bestowed its name,
which made a generous living along its shores,
has long been consigned to the disrespect
of grease, sewage, and detergents,
and is now adorned with a floating casino.

Long ago in a strange and unhappy time,
it was the Fox that brought me comfort,
my companion in every season,
from ragged ice to still waters in August
the flowing stream a great calendar,
marked by the birds in their seasons,
and the motions of muskrats and fish.

Without the river's good company,
our father's final years would have been grimmer.
Its banks provided the peace of fishing,
respite from a lifetime of worries,
an escape from difficult conclusions,
and in death, he elected to stay nearby,
near the current's endless passing,
not a bad place to spend eternity.

Chicago

As we arrived from Dixie in 1951,
a walk in the Loop and lunch at the Berghof
were only the first act in the show.
There were huge buildings and miles of train yards,
the museums and Marshall Field's,
the zoo, the El, and the aquarium,
and on the South Side, the White Sox.

In the city, alien worlds sat side by side.
The bums outside Pacific Garden Mission
were shambling just two narrow blocks
from the luxury of Michigan Avenue,
and a few lanes of traffic and Comiskey Park
separated Irish Bridgeport and the mayor
from the sullen towers of the Taylor Homes.

The movie theaters were a marvel,
where the shows began at 9:00 a.m.;
there were diners that never closed,
newsstands with papers in unknown languages,
magazines with anatomy lessons,
and the happy chaos of New Year's Eve
at the corner of State and Randolph.

Long ago, in pursuit of true love,
I memorized twenty miles of subway stations
and pledged my eternal devotion to her
outside the doors of Symphony Hall
with a penny ring bought on Wabash Avenue.
Sadly enough, the Berghof is no more,
and I am long gone to other places,
but I can still hear all the songs.

Chicago: The Early Years

Unlike many people who lived in Aurora, we spent a lot of time in Chicago. Our father worked there (when he was not abroad), knew the city well, and had introduced our mother to the advantages of shopping in the Loop almost immediately after we moved to Aurora in 1951. In her mind, Chicago was a resource not to be overlooked. Block and Kuhl's in Aurora might be convenient, but compared to Marshall Field & Co., it was strictly minor league.

Why did so few people from Aurora partake of the joys of Chicago—a mere forty miles away? Strange as it seemed to us, a good piece of this reluctance was probably fear. Many people in Aurora were certain a visit to Chicago would result in being the victim of some heinous crime. I had many high school classmates who had never set foot in the big city. Another group had only been on some specific excursion to one of the ballparks or to a place like Riverview (an amusement park). I knew hardly anyone of my age who was as familiar with the Loop, the museums and the other attractions as I was.

From an early age, we regularly found ourselves seated in one of the coaches of the CB&Q's suburban service. Even today, almost fifty years since I last rode on one of these trains, I can still rattle off the names of most every stop between Aurora and Chicago. There were some twenty or so possible stops but at least half a dozen were all but abandoned. It was always a thrill, though, to be on one of the trains that stopped at a seldom served place like Clyde, Harlem or Western Avenue. The best part of the trip was the last stretch before the end of the line as we passed through an enormous freight yard and counted as many different rail line logos as possible. There was nothing quite like the resonance of those names: The Nickel Plate Road, the Monon, The Gulf, Mobile and Ohio, or The Seaboard Air Line.

Depending on how many stops the train made, travel time might vary between forty-five minutes and an hour and fifteen minutes. Even during the off hours, the service was frequent and convenient.

The trip ended at Union Station, Chicago's busiest terminal and a grand palace from the glory days of rail travel. The station itself was a major attraction as far as my brother and I were concerned. It was crowded at all hours (and lots of the people were good watching), had interesting shops, and the mysterious Semaphore, another one of those dark drinking establishments that offered the allure of sin and decadence. Nothing fueled imagination like all those track boards listing trains to so many distant and wonderful cities.

Every shopping trip to Chicago with Mother involved the Marshall Field store at the corner of Randolph and State. While we might stop at Carson's occasionally, we did not patronize the other department stores. The Fair, Goldblatt's, Mandel's and Wieboldt's thus all remained a mystery for the most part.

Marshall Field was an amazing place. The main store was composed of three separate but connected buildings and occupied an entire city block. Across Washington Street was a fourth building that housed the Store for Men. You could buy anything you needed at Field's, from clothing to curtains or flags to fireplace tongs. In its heyday, it had a book department that was larger than most bookstores, the best selection of fabrics and dry goods in the city, an extensive stamp and coin department, an enormous gallery of oriental rugs, and even a department that bought and sold rare antiques. At Christmas time there was a special attraction: the first-floor window galleries were turned over to an elaborate and beautifully decorated Christmas story. Starting with the window designated number one, you circled the building as the story spun out (portrayed by mannequins and told on storyboards) until you reached the finale that usually featured some gloriously happy family sitting in front of the hearth. At some point old St. Nick would make the mandatory appearance.

It was a store that excelled in service. Field's salespeople were legendary for their expertise in their product offerings. Any purchase could be delivered at no charge to anywhere in the Chicago area; thus, our mother did not have to schlepp her bags back on the train. In the early years, it even offered free childcare to the mother who wanted to be able to shop without having to supervise her brood. This was no doubt quite attractive to Nelle Bourgo who had a very energetic preschooler on her hands (my brother) and even had resorted to a harness arrangement to keep the little tyke in tow when we were in Chicago, where the enormous crowds could quickly swallow a small child.

Within the store, there were at least six separate eating places ranging from snacks and ice cream to elegant dining rooms that served full meals. My brother and I had a strong preference: the English Room, where our favorite offering was a roast beef platter incongruously called the "Paul Bunyan Special." Sadly enough, the *mater* was partial to the Walnut Room and not always willing to be persuaded to take us to the English Room. However, she usually made certain we got a few minutes to look over the toy department, which was fully stocked throughout the year in an era when most stores offered a large selection of toys only for the Christmas season. It was loaded with marvelous stuff we knew we'd never own—but one could always hope.

Not every visit was for shopping. Several times a year we would get in a trip to a museum, or in the summers a visit to the zoo. Our favorite museum by far was the Museum of Science and Industry, which featured among its many wonders a simulated coal mine complete with a ride on a mine tram, a German U-Boat captured in WWII, an incredible pendulum suspended through several stories, and the most wonderful model train we had ever seen. Jon and I were also fond of the Aquarium, but the Planetarium did not click (as an adult, I found it much more rewarding). Our father loved the visual arts (his book collection included numerous art books) but for some reason, we spent little time at the Art Institute, and likewise, I only started to appreciate it during my adult years.

We also visited various expositions and fairs. I recall "Powerama" – an enormous event put on by GM in 1955 that featured some 250 exhibits of their various products. We liked it so much we persuaded Mom to take us back for an encore visit a few weeks later. Like many other attractions of that day, it was free. Museums charged no admission in those days and the Brookfield Zoo was also free. Today, a family of four would pay more than $70 just to park the family car and gain admission to the zoo.

There was no end to the attractions to which our mother might take her boys. She was curious and willing to give anything a try. Beyond an old favorite like the circus, we tried rodeos and a water-skiing show. We even went to car and boat shows just to gawk (since there was no chance our family would ever own either), and I recall my brother and I were very taken with the "Henry J," one of the models introduced during the decade-long effort by the Kaiser Corporation to establish itself in the auto market. One summer when I was away at scout camp, she took my brother to attend a Wild West Show at Wrigley Field starring the Lone Ranger and Tonto. I was not pleased to discover I had missed a chance to see two of my favorite heroes.

Much of the wonder of Chicago was simply walking the streets. The crowds were enormous and always in a hurry. On Wabash or Lake Street, the El roared and rattled overhead as we walked along. At every corner, there were lines of green and white CTA buses going to such exotic places as Hyde Park, Ravenswood, and Blue Island. There were enormous newsstands with more magazines and newspapers than we would have imagined possible. The specialty merchandisers were a favorite for window shopping: nothing like getting to see dozens of different sorts of knives, scissors and barber tools at a place called Corrado Cutlery, pipes and other smoking gear at Dunhill's, or fountain pens, pencils, drafting tools and so forth at a specialty stationery store.

Once in a while we would stay until quitting time at Harza Engineering and either collect Dad at his office or meet at a restaurant where we would have supper before going back to Aurora. We often went to a Chicago chain restaurant called Toffinetti's, which had a location in the Union Station and several in the Loop. On special occasions, we might get to go to the Berghof (nothing quite like that chopped sirloin steak). It was the first place we went to eat upon arrival from the South in 1951 and remained my personal favorite until it closed in 2008. (It has recently reopened, but my brother tells me the new place is only a shadow of its former self.)

Tofinetti's, though, was the scene of an episode that remained a source of merriment in our family for many years. One night we were seated next to an older gent who was eating alone. He was plainly in a disagreeable mood, and the waiter responded in turn with lackluster service. At some point, the waiter delivered an order of toast, but it was quite burned, almost black. The customer was outraged and demanded the waiter replace his order. When the waiter refused, the customer ostentatiously held up a piece of the toast and started to scrape it clean with his knife. Our father was much amused and we started to giggle. Naturally enough, our mother could not conceal her annoyance with all three of us for our egregious violation of public decorum. It was most unusual for her to reveal any disapproval of her spouse. (We, of course, were a different matter.)

Thereafter, from time to time, one of the three Bourgo males would go through a pantomime of the drama involving the toast. It was often invoked in response to some sob story, and it would always get a laugh from the audience—though Nelle would always shake her head and pretend to disapprove.

The Ceremonies of Life

The apartment where we lived from 1951 to 1954 in Aurora, Illinois, had several distinct advantages. The building was set on what seemed a huge lot, which meant we had plenty of space for games and adventures. There was a horse chestnut in the back with branches low enough to climb and each fall it produced a large supply of projectiles, handy to have when an available target might present itself. Behind the tree was a long row of overgrown lilacs, spirea, and other ornamentals that was a perfect place for the bandits to hide out if cowboys and Indians were the order of the day.

The house sat on a corner formed by Downer Place and an alley named Hawthorne Court that extended one block north to Galena Boulevard. Hawthorne was poorly drained, which meant a decent rain would produce a most useful body of water just a few steps from our front door. We would then have a temporary venue for naval exercises considerably beyond the dimensions of the bathtub.

Socially, this was also an excellent place to live. Within a block of our home, there were at least two dozen other children, most of them grade schoolers like me or preschoolers like my brother. This meant that on almost any foray outside playmates were instantly available. There was also a sprinkling of older sisters who excelled at leadership and whose directions we were eager to follow.

Lastly, we lived on the opposite side of the street from the large and busy Our Savior Lutheran church and just a short block west of the Healy Funeral Chapel. Both institutions were valuable sources of entertainment, especially in the warmer months when we could sit on the front steps and watch the varied activities that unrolled at each location, though in the case of Healy we might walk down to the corner to get a closer peek at the goings-on.

The major diversions at Our Savior were the Saturday afternoon weddings that seemed to occur on a frequent basis. Marriage must have been popular among Lutherans in the early 1950s; on some Saturdays, there might be two. My brother and I stared at the wedding party (mostly at the bride, I am sure) and all their finery in genial ignorance until one of our neighborhood girls took us in hand and started filling us in on the details. It was Libby Coleson, a sassy and opinionated type who lived in the other apartment off our landing, and who usually wrote off the Bourgo boys as hopelessly uninformed. Jon and I, likewise, had little regard for her, but at times she was a useful person to know.

We did find her parents glamorous. Her mother was beautiful, we thought—almost a movie star—and her father, though, shorter than our father by some 6 inches, came off as quite the dashing fellow, always impeccably dressed. Bud and Mary Coleson were also the owners of a 1950 Chevy coupe, while we were the perpetual odd ducks with no personal transportation aside from our tricycles.

With our fleet of vehicles, summer 1952.

Libby instructed us in all the particulars of weddings. People were throwing rice at the happy couple as they emerged from the church but the reasons for this were unclear. At some point, the bride would toss her bouquet to some lucky girl, who would be the next to get married. The bride and groom were leaving for some mysterious journey called a honeymoon and could only get there in a car which had been decorated in outlandish fashion including tin cans attached to the rear bumper. Some couples thought it was a good idea to cruise around town for a while after the wedding, blowing the horn and waving at everyone, even at small boys they did not know.

This was all a good deal to absorb. Neither Jon nor I saw being married as an especially lucky or desirable state. Several of our adult male role models were unmarried, which we found to be admirable, and like many siblings, we had firm plans to stick together throughout life and never to marry. We made solemn promises, much to the amusement of both parents. Our biases about matrimony were confirmed by the saga of Bud and Mary Coleman. At some point Bud mysteriously disappeared from the scene, leaving Mary and the girls on their own. After we left the building in 1954, we lost touch with them. We later heard both had left Aurora and ultimately divorced.

The funeral home was a less reliable and predictable source of diversions. Events took place less often and sometimes at inconvenient hours—while I was in school or at night. We did not have a reliable mentor like Libby to provide commentary, so we were not always sure what was going on, but we were entirely aware a dead body was involved—and we all wanted to be on hand to see the casket coming out the front door and into the hearse. It wasn't difficult to understand that this was not a happy event, but that certainly did not dampen our curiosity. There was a general agreement it would be quite the thing to get to ride in a car with one of those little purple banners—a parade sometimes led by a policeman!

From an early age, our mother believed in letting us play outside on our own, though within well-defined boundaries. Confident of both her authority and her instruction, she rarely found it necessary to come outside to see what we were up to. One time, though, she emerged to find a group of us down at the corner, gawking at the solemn happenings across the street. This was absolutely contrary to her firmest beliefs, and in no time she had rounded up the gang and had us marching quickstep back home.

For Mother, the rules of courtesy and consideration ranked very close to her basic ethical values—in fact, they were simply a different part of the moral landscape. Respect for other people's privacy and dignity were pounded into both of us from our earliest days, and she made it utterly clear that she would have expected me to know that staring at a funeral procession was outside the pale.

We knew that she rarely came out, so we were probably not too worried when succumbing to temptation the next time, but her fury, flavored with touches of her Southern roots, was a formidable thing, and I will imagine that we were smart enough to watch from a more discreet distance.

413 Downer Place (1952)

We had come to live in a strange town,
where we were teased on the playground,
our Southern voices ringing alien,
but were soon encircled by other children,
and found the natural order of the street
in the parade of wagons and tricycles
that patrolled from Chestnut to Wilder.

Home was upstairs in a rambling old house
that had been converted to apartments,
ours made cozy and comfortable
by our mother's loving but casual style;
conveniently located on the Downer route,
we could stand in the front yard each evening
and wait for Dad to alight from the bus.

It had all the needs of two small boys:
a lawn generous enough for ball games
and a horse chestnut with low branches,
a long stand of lilacs where outlaws hid,
an alley rarely traveled by cars,
and friends with plenty of older sisters
who always seemed to have good ideas.

It was here we learned to walk to school,
carried pop bottles back to the Jewel Tea,
sat on the lawn at the New England Church
and counted the trucks on US 30,
strolled down the hill to the yards
where the EJ&E sorted out freight cars;
and when the old dog died,
it was good to be going to a new house.

Lunch with Father

My brother Jon and I spent most of our childhood in a single parent setting, managed by a busy and authoritative mother. Our father had launched a career as a project manager in an engineering firm whose major efforts were overseas, principally in the Middle East. As befitted a man who came of age in the 1930s, he put work at the top of the agenda and was routinely at work sites abroad for as much as nine months out of the year throughout our entire childhood.

As a result, we led two entirely different lifestyles as children. When he was absent, the cuisine leaned to the Southern style cooking our Tennessee-born mother preferred. Dinner was informal and often consumed in the kitchen. When our father was around, the menu was Midwest basic, served formally in the dining room and the portions were substantial. Our mother cooked two pork chops for each person. It wasn't a meal worthy of the name, in her opinion, if it did not offer at least two vegetables in addition to potatoes, rolls, and a salad.

It would be hard to exaggerate how different our eating habits were in those days. "Salad" encompassed a lot more than lettuce and other raw vegetables tossed with a modicum of dressing. If lettuce was featured, it was iceberg lettuce, served in a wedge and covered with 1000 island dressing. Other elements in the "salad" entry included cream cheese, cottage cheese, canned fruit, and Jell-O in many different forms. Our mother favored fruit cocktail in red Jell-O and canned pears in the green variety.

Organ meats such as liver were commonly consumed in perfect innocence of their now proclaimed lethal quantities of cholesterol. Liver was in fact often served with bacon and sausage on the side, known as a "mixed grill." Vegetables were—by today's standards—overcooked and soggy, always supplemented with butter or sauce. In our home at least, pasta (save macaroni and cheese) was never prepared for a meal. Instead, spaghetti was something out of a can you might get for lunch.

If Dad was around, Saturday lunch was a special time. It was the only day of the week we shared the noon meal with him. During the week he was in Chicago at the office, and Sunday, we observed the fast before church (even though we did not go to a Catholic church), a vestige of our father's boyhood spent in a high church Episcopal parish with occasional sojourns among his Catholic relations. Consequently, Sunday fare was brunch after church, and later in the afternoon, the traditional Sunday dinner served around three o'clock.

Lunch on Saturday was typically the standard fare mother served up most days—various sandwiches and Campbell's soup being her mainstays. Occasionally, Dad would request a meal I have always thought of as the "spread," an elaborate buffet of all sorts of items he considered great delicacies. Today's gourmets would be horrified by the items he loved, as they were neither fresh nor local, but came largely out of cans. Jon and I were always fascinated with the locales from which these items came—Norway, Spain, Demark, and occasionally someplace as exotic as Morocco.

The centerpiece of this feast was a loaf of dense, chewy German pumpernickel bread, sliced very thin (8 slices to the inch or so), which our father would spread with butter or cream cheese. On the top went sardines, anchovies, smoked oysters, capers, pimientos, and various other ingredients. Accompanying the main course would be a half dozen varieties of pickles, black and green olives, cottage cheese, potato salad, radishes, and celery sticks. Dad was a purist when it came to condiments: even when he ventured into Danish canned ham, he never used mayonnaise, mustard or the like. He did have a great fondness for horseradish and it was always on hand.

My brother and I were fascinated by this operation, watching the old man construct his series of open-face sandwiches from the various ingredients on the table. I was a bolder eater than Jon, and occasionally essayed a nibble only to discover nothing had changed: I still did not like anchovies, either flat or rolled. I did fancy the celery if stuffed with Kraft cheese from a jar, which was also a regular part of this operation. I can't recall what our mother ate, but my memory is that she was not nearly as enthusiastic about these offerings as our father, and Jon and I, naturally, had something more suited to our tastes.

The other aspect of these exotic lunches was the occasional shopping trip to gather the ingredients. This took place at Stein's, a vigorous enterprise located at the corner of Galena Boulevard and River Street near downtown Aurora, Illinois, perhaps a half mile from the apartment where we lived at the time. As our parents never owned a car and Stein's was considered too close to justify bus fare, we walked both ways.

It is not easy to say what Stein's was. Like many family operations, it was a collection of businesses that grew incrementally over the years, as the family thought of new ventures to add. It was not a grocery store, although it did have a few convenience items such as milk, eggs, snacks, and bread. It was not merely a delicatessen, either, although the store did have various and sundry cold cuts and cheeses and several genuine pickle barrels. It had a large selection of beer ("Over 90 Brands of Bottled Beer," proclaimed a sign), and a spacious liquor department. Stein's offered select fresh meats and was probably the only place in Aurora with fresh fish. And there was a row of aisles Dad loved to peruse, which had all the various canned specialty items he so enjoyed at those lunches.

What I remember most powerfully about the place was the smell—it had a pungent, slightly sour odor, the smell of a place that handled a lot of perishables, but before the days when every effort was made to suppress it. I recalled the place at once the first time I was in Europe years later when visiting food stores that made no attempt to conceal what business they were in.

The other feature of Stein's was Norman himself—the son of the founder, an energetic and garrulous man who presided at the fish counter, and who was always ready for a chat with a favorite customer. Our father and Norman appeared to have little in common aside from an interest in food, but they had grown up in the same neighboring town of Joliet, and their conversations (at least to two small boys) seemed to go on forever. As the talk droned on, we despaired, having already completed our inspection of the fish and our tour through the varieties of Reese's Finer Foods, S. S. Pierce canned delicacies, and the many Cross and Blackwell soups.

Finally, it was time to complete the transaction and head home, which itself was a treat. The first leg took us along the louche east side of South River Street. The west side was the polite side— Sylvester's Café, the hardware store, and the Old Second National Bank, but we got to pass and peek into John's Smoke Shop (Pool and Plate Lunches) and one of the bars. Turning right at Downer place, we could look across the street at the curious mysteries of Ray's Spider Web, another of the bars in downtown Aurora. Ray's promised a unique form of sin, with a name that stirred our thoughts.

Crossing Lake Street we passed the Jewel Tea and started up the hill, now on the home stretch. The first block was long and shady, almost dark from the dense covering of elms over the street. It featured a house with a big sign in front identifying it as an accordion school. My brother and I found this place the sort of mystery that was always good for a conversation. During all our years in the neighborhood, we never saw anyone coming or going into the place. What was going on in this alleged school? (Whatever the enterprise, the sign was there for many years.)

Past Locust Street, the trees thinned out and we were back in the sun as we passed the Healy Funeral Chapel and once across Chestnut Street, our apartment was in the second house. On the way home my brother and I no doubt engaged in one of the games one used for diversion on strolls (perhaps trying to make sure we did not step on cracks or in squares with the builders name stamped in the concrete), and if we even thought about what was for dinner, I am sure we were relieved it would not be any of that stuff our father was carrying in our mother's prized brown canvas shopping bag.

Easter Greetings

At ages seven and four, most likely, and probably taken at
Marshall Field's in Chicago. As you've already noted our
mother was very keen on matching outfits.

The Engineer (1915-1979)

He escaped from his father's cautious world
where a desire to emulate his heroes
(Astaire and Twain) had been flattened:
no dancing, no steamboats, but engineering.
In '37 he went South, a newly made BSCE,
working on FDR's payroll at the TVA,
and the wick of ambition was lit.

War and recovery made seven years vanish,
but he was ready for the moment,
hired as employee number five in a firm
that he helped to grow into hundreds.
He followed the work around the world,
from the Snake to the Tigris to the Indus,
at home in the bush and the board room.

Al took possession of what no one wanted:
his colleagues loved to design and devise
while he worried about costs and completion dates.
His projects drew attention and won awards,
he floated to the top of the pile,
vice president and area manager at forty,
while wife and sons waited at home.

He was slowed by an early heart attack,
delegated the field work to his proteges,
and finished his climb to the top,
at last the chief, but irreparably damaged.
The commander learned to reign instead of rule,
took up fishing and flowers on Saturdays,
and waited for the inexorable verdict
with more calm than those who loved him.

Mary A. Todd School: Matters Academic

I can't think of any institution more important in our childhood than the small public grade school in our neighborhood. It was apparently not named for Lincoln's wife, but a beloved Aurora teacher. Todd was a two-story brick building put up by the WPA in the 1930s, complete with the WPA arts project murals of American historical scenes on the walls.

The school was laid out into four or five classrooms on each story, a principal's office in an annex off the staircase to the second floor, and a gymnasium attached to the rear. Grades kindergarten through third were on the first floor along with an art room. The second floor housed the upper grades plus the school library. The basement held the locker rooms for gym class, the furnace, and a workroom for our school janitor, Mr. Sinclair. Behind the gymnasium was a large asphalt playground complete with basketball hoops and two painted baseball diamonds.

Presiding over this institution was a genial and kindly man named Charles A. Friday. Unlike the school principals of today, Mr. Friday was not blessed with a staff of specialists. His team consisted of Mr. Sinclair and a secretary, who amazed us with her ability to type on a machine without letters on the keys and who doubled as medic when presented with a scrape or a bloody nose. I have nothing but fond memories of her and quite unjustly cannot recollect her name.

As a man of many demeanors, Mr. Friday was well suited for his role. He was, as the situation demanded it, a good listener, a stern policeman, and a judicious arbitrator. He doled out praise when he thought it deserved and malfeasance was never allowed to pass unnoticed. Whenever he decided to give the playground a look during recess, we all took heed and knew it was time to stay on the straight and narrow. I can still recall that great feeling of relief when he approached me. and it was only to say hello—and not some reprimand for an infraction I could not remember committing. Since our mother was a school activist, she and Mr. Friday were well-acquainted; thus, I had to be doubly careful.

In my first few years at Todd, the school somehow managed to house grades seven and eight, as Aurora did not yet have junior high schools. In fall 1953, as I was entering the fourth grade, the new high school opened and the old high school was transformed into Franklin Junior High School. From that point on Todd began to add extra sections of the lower grades as the baby boomers (including my dear brother) began to invade the hallowed halls. By the time I left in 1956, the place was beginning to burst at the seams. Any extra space like the art room and a portion of the library was turned into classrooms. Desks spilled out of the classrooms and into the cloakrooms as class sizes swelled.

Sixth Grade with Miss Faircloth dated January 27, 1956. Looks like a free reading or study period since she is at her desk.

Our teachers were fittingly the stars of the show. Some we positively adored, some we admired, and others might make us nervous, but I never doubted their authority or their qualifications to be leading me in the paths of knowledge. Reflecting the pre-war years (when married women were not allowed to teach primary grades) four of my teachers were unmarried women, one on the younger side, two middle-aged, and one venerable figure, Miss Randall, who was nearing the end of a long and illustrious career. I believe my class was either her last or next to last before she retired. There was also Mr. Williams, our fifth-grade teacher, the rare man found in the primary grades, who doubled as the coach for our sports teams and as a gym teacher for the fifth and sixth grades.

Expectations of our intellectual progress were more modest than today. I never went to kindergarten, but my impression is that it was mostly about learning to socialize and sit still. We did not really begin to read until second grade. First grade focused on learning the alphabet, forming the letters, and mastering the reading and writing of a few short and simple phrases. By the time we got to fourth grade, we were subjected to all the various and sundry exercises associated with learning classic Palmer script. In keeping with my general ineptitude in the graphic arts, handwriting was never one of my best skills. I can still see Mrs. Blubaum shaking her head as she perused my tortured scribbles.

We were very much in the era of Dick and Jane. As we have all subsequently realized, the books presented a terribly distorted view of the country. The mother did not work and the father obviously had a white-collar job of some sort. The faces were all white and life was swell in every way. Of course, many of us found these images completely congruent with what we witnessed most days. My chief objection to the books was that I thought they were too easy and dull stuff compared to what I read at home.

By the third grade or so we encountered the regular pleasure of the *Weekly Reader*, a four-page periodical distributed throughout the country. There was an edition for each grade level and the articles introduced us to geography, current events, science, and other worthy topics. At some point at the end of the week, there might be a quiz (no doubt helpfully furnished by the publisher) to determine if we had mastered the information in that week's issue. It was always a point of pride for me to achieve 100 on this exercise and most weeks I managed to do that. As I was already reading newspapers and almanacs, perhaps I had an unfair edge.

Spelling got a great deal of attention. Then as now (at least at my grandchildren's school) the weekly spelling list of twenty words or so and the Friday quiz were as regular as clockwork. Each day we spent some portion of time going over the words, getting counsel on the tricky ones like "answer," and being called to the blackboard to write them, all in preparation for that ultimate test at the end of the week. As with any examination, the competition to finish at 100% and get the sticker was brisk, and the winners were not always gracious to the losers. On math tests, an additional point of pride was to finish first in addition to getting all the problems right, though the temptation to rush hindered accuracy.

I do not recall we spent a great deal of time on science, though in fifth grade we got a good deal of exposure to the natural world. Mr. Williams scheduled field trips, where he introduced me to the world of bird watching, which became a lifelong interest. His class also provided the thrill of live animals in our classroom including newts, snakes and a pair of guinea pigs, who added to the general excitement by providing us with a litter of babies. There was a lottery for the young ones at the end of the school year and I was one of the losers—just as well since I knew our mother would have refused entry to such a creature. Otherwise, science was largely anecdotal with occasional oohs and ahs while the teacher poured vinegar into baking powder and made it foam.

History did not get a lot of scrutiny, either, except around certain holidays like Columbus Day, Armistice Day, Thanksgiving or in February, when Washington and Lincoln's birthday were celebrated by reading or listening to stories about great figures from the American past. We all loved Lincoln's birthday and Armistice Day because both were school holidays in Illinois. For years I lived in happy ignorance of what "armistice" meant. What difference did it make? We got the day off.

Once a week or so we would get a visit from the art teacher and joined Mrs. McDonald in the art room where we attempted to learn how to draw, paint, cut out designs for paper collages and make figures out of clay. Whatever talents I had were more a matter of enthusiasm than skill, and I envied those classmates who produced professional looking results.

The music teacher also made a weekly appearance and led us through some lusty, if not tuneful, renditions of Steven Foster songs and other old favorites. We all enjoyed our fourth-grade year with Mrs. Blubaum, because she was a music enthusiast, played the piano and so, we got an extra songfest in every so often. In matters musical, one of the saints had to be Harry "Pops" Nigro, the district teacher for instrumental music. In the fourth grade, we were eligible to choose an instrument and begin group instruction. Few of us had either the talent or the industry required to master an instrument, but Pops was a jovial realist who never badgered the slackers about not practicing. He was contented enough that one or two students in ten managed to learn enough to be in the band or orchestra. That did not include me—my brief encounter with the violin was a flop.

Geography was a serious subject and by fourth grade or so, it was a topic that got daily attention. We were expected to learn the states, foreign countries, and their capital cities. There was an infinite number of lakes, rivers, and oceans whose names we were to commit to memory. We watched an endless stream of film strips (a sort of slide show) about daily life in China, the Arctic, and other exotic places. I can recall a survey of Europe in which we were introduced to the major products of each country and I wondered what the Germans did with all that potash. Two of our classmates were from European refugee families, one from Norway (Robert) and the other from somewhere in Russia (Neal). Robert, one of the class scholars, eagerly talked at length about the life and customs of Norway. When prompted, Neal had little to say about Russia, except that his parents were not eager to return—which only confirmed our suspicions about the USSR.

School at Todd was about mastering the basic facts and skills. Unlike some stories I have heard from others of my age, we did not have school assemblies to direct our little minds away from the lure of Communism (that was unfortunately not true in high school). We did not have to take patriotism classes and pass muster on our knowledge of what was superior in capitalism and Christianity. We were certainly aware of the Cold War and our nation's disagreements with the USSR, but the issues were not pounded into our heads. We did sing patriotic songs such as *America the Beautiful* and *My Country 'Tis of Thee,* but not the *Star-Spangled Banner.* It had only been the national anthem for twenty-five years and was perhaps thought too difficult for grade schoolers to sing. Students also recited the Pledge of Allegiance each morning, but otherwise, no great emphasis was placed on national pride. Patriotism was assumed to be the norm.

When the polio vaccine became generally available about 1955, the school system was a major partner in organizing the mass inoculation of young children. We were all marched class by class to the nearby Catholic grade school where we got our shot. It was a great relief to me that Dr. Salk had figured this problem out. Though I never had any close friend who got seriously ill from polio, it was a genuine anxiety of those times—the effects could be devastating, and the pages of *Life* made me more than aware of its dreadful consequences. Some years (no doubt thanks of the generosity of the Federal Government and skills of the American farmer) we all got a free carton of surplus milk every morning. At other times, the district nurse would drop by and dose us with cod liver oil capsules, a vast improvement over the liquid variety administered at home.

It is sometimes fashionable to characterize the public schools of that and earlier eras as Protestant academies with public funding. One hears tales of prayer in school, stories from the Bible and other anecdotes that portray the school as a sectarian arena where Jews and Catholics (let alone Muslims and Hindus) would have felt unwelcome unless they conformed to the norms of the majority. This was not the case at Mary A. Todd. We never prayed and the enthusiast who wanted to witness was gently steered off topic by the teacher. Thanksgiving was treated as a matter of national history and the closest we got to Easter might be an egg or a rabbit sticker on a spelling test in early spring. Granted, we did sing Christmas songs as the great day approached in December, but Baby Jesus got the cold shoulder in favor of Rudolph and one-horse sleighs.

Second grade at Mary A. Todd in the spring of 1952. The occasion was a class project investigating how bread came to be, culminating in a dramatic presentation for our parents in the school gym. The author is the first guy in the third row from the right, holding a pointer he used in his exalted role as the narrator. The girl on the left end of the first row makes another appearance on page 208.

Mrs. Blubaum

In fourth grade, I had my first teacher
who was not a secular nun
but married, with a life outside school,
who discussed her husband and children,
a brisk classroom manager
who taught all the usual subjects,
and that learning was serious business.

She was the first to acknowledge
that we had made some progress
in our long march towards competence,
disdaining the reward of seasonal stickers
on successful math papers or spelling tests,
noting instead succinct congratulations
written perfectly in red fountain pen ink.

Mrs. B. directed the recess softball game,
taking the mound in skirt and heels,
both steady pitcher and umpire,
tossing a stream of strikes and encouragement,
a favorite acolyte positioned nearby
to handle throws and ground balls
since her role did not include fielding.

The woman believed in continuous improvement,
her favorite words, "We can do better"
often heard when I had missed some target,
but they always came with a smile,
and I would walk back to my desk
with feelings of pride and excitement,
a man with a difficult mission
who was prepared to give it his all.

Mary A. Todd: Matters Social

Unlike my brother, an authentic baby boomer, I sailed through these years as a member of a modestly populated bunch—those born in the latter years of the war. Consequently, I spent all six years of grade school with the same group of people. There were a few changes over the years, but we got to know each other quite well and by the sixth grade our roles were well understood, and our identities as class clown, geek, social director, athlete, wise guy, glamor girl, etc., were well established. Some of us were reliable and some of us were careless. Some of us were little saints (at least in public) and some of us were always looking for an excuse.

We were not a diverse group in terms of race or ethnicity. There were a few blacks living in the district, but African-American children were shunted off to another grade school. From time to time, the children of migrant Mexican farm laborers would appear, but they never stayed for long. Since most of our Catholic peers attended Holy Angels School, our school was largely white and Protestant. In Aurora in the 1950s, Protestants and Catholics tended to live in separate social circles. The few Catholic boys I met in my grade school years were mostly the ones I encountered at the YMCA. It was not until 9th grade that I made many Catholic acquaintances. There was a Catholic high school for the girls at that point, but for various reasons, some parents opted for the public high school. The only option for the boys was a somewhat unpopular military academy that many families found uncongenial.

We did go to high school and junior high with our black peers, though I can't believe it could have been a pleasant experience for them. They were a very small group and surely felt ill at ease in a sea of white faces—moreover, white faces with no concept of how demeaning their country made life for minority populations. There was little doubt the boys were encouraged by the school administration to drop out once they reached 16. By the time my class graduated there were perhaps a half dozen black girls and one solitary boy remaining.

At Mary A. Todd we were a diverse group in terms of our socioeconomic backgrounds. Two of our fathers were engineers, another was a local merchant, and several were teachers. For a while, one of our classmates was the son of a Methodist minister. Two girls were from wealthy families, connected with two of the leading manufacturing firms in town. We also had the son of a car mechanic, children whose fathers worked in one of the many local factories, and several who had to deal with the opprobrium of living with a single working mother. It was a different world in terms of attitudes towards divorce. Adlai Stevenson offended many voters in 1952 because he was the first divorced man to run for the Presidency. There were also some concerns about his religious affiliation (he was a Unitarian) but less than one might hear in certain quarters these days.

Todd was not a large district, but in those days people did not live in the sorts of enclaves that are common today. One block might be a little seedy and the next quite upscale. Within the district were several collections of fine homes just a few doors away from apartments or more modest houses. Our school also included several blocks of marginal housing on the edge of downtown and encompassed the walk-up apartments on several commercial streets along the west end of the business district. Our own apartment was a half block east of the Copley Mansion, which was usually acknowledged to be the number one dwelling in Aurora. Proximity to affluent neighbors was a distinct advantage on Halloween night.

I suppose I should have noticed the difference in the ways we dressed for school, but in truth, I don't recall I ever picked up any signals in that regard. More telling were other matters. Every class had a mimeographed list of students (including the parents' names and telephone numbers) that was passed out in class with instructions to take it home. I couldn't help but notice that a few people had no telephone number noted and there were several with a mother or father with a *different* last name. Today such practices would violate all sorts of policies, but in those days privacy concerns were minimal.

Another event that must have caused a certain amount of discomfort or a feeling of being left out was the Scholastic book sale. Periodically, the teacher would pass out a Scholastic catalog of books available for sale. The next step was to take the catalog home and negotiate with one's parent over how many items could be had. Our mother usually set something like a $2.00 limit on our purchases, but since no book cost more than 35 cents, I could usually figure how to get at least a half dozen or so promising titles in my favorite categories: science fiction, *Ripley's Believe It or Not*, baseball and jokes. On the great day when the books arrived there were always classmates who watched the rest of us with envy as we delighted in our new possessions.

Today the schools are more careful about how this is done. Scholastic still has book sales at schools, but the procedure is now to ship a large selection of books to a participating school, which then holds a book fair in the gymnasium on a weekend. As might be expected, my grandchildren are always careful to make sure I know the date of the great event.

Still, other things divided us up. Our district was almost entirely urban, but there were a small number of rural students who came to school on the bus. For some reason, instead of sending these children to one school, or to the nearest school, they were sprinkled around the district. Their assignments were apparently determined by available space. As a result, most of these children never knew where they might end up from year to year. One farm boy I made friends with in fourth grade had been to four schools in four years, and sure enough, he was not with us for the fifth grade.

Todd, like all the grade schools in District 129, had no lunch room or food service. Almost all of us walked home at noon to eat lunch and then set off back to school again. Working parents who could not be home could send their child to school with a lunch that was eaten in the gymnasium under the supervision of the janitor. Since our mother was a busy soul with many irons in the community fires, she occasionally dispatched us to school with a sack lunch and a note asking leave for us to eat our sandwich at school. I knew that certain children always felt a little stigmatized by being in the "lunch" crowd, but my brother and I liked the arrangement. After eating lunch, we were turned out on the playground for an extra period of recess.

Unlike many parents, our mother was open and candid about the matter of economic inequality. Jon and I were made aware from an early age that we were a fortunate pair and that we ought to be thankful. Nelle was thoroughly egalitarian and she expected the same of us. Money had nothing to do with character or worth and she spent a lifetime making friends with people of every conceivable sort and rank. At some point, Jon and I met a boy whose mother was the housekeeper in one of the grand places up the block. Nelle befriended that woman during their brief stay, and she was likely one of the few women in the neighborhood who did.

She never hesitated to push us in that direction, too. I won't say she insisted I make friends with the boy who lived with his grandmother (neither of his parents wanted him), but when I asked if I could bring him home one day after school, her enthusiasm was palpable. The after-school snack that afternoon was more sumptuous than usual.

For the most part, I was the classically obedient student. Thanks to that stern moralist, Nelle C. Bourgo, I was prone to think carefully about the right thing to do. I do recall one day when I strayed, much to my regret. On that day one of our unfortunates had worn some article of clothing to school the class bully thought laughable. He managed to round up several disciples on the playground before school started, and the bunch started throwing out names and other insults. Somehow, I could not resist the temptation to join in the fun. Perhaps it was because I (round, bespectacled, and a hopeless athlete) was often a target myself and was happy, for once, to be on the sending side.

Our victim was not quite as passive as might have been wished. He complained to the venerable Miss Randall and I, along with several others, was fingered for the crime. To this day I am not sure which was worse—staying after school under her censorious eye to write "I will never call someone names again" twenty-five times—or having to explain to the maternal authority why I was a half hour late coming home from school. The school had already called to report my infraction, but our mother was masterful at the art of showing spontaneous disappointment in my performance. I was at least smart enough to know there was no point in trying to conceal or excuse my disgrace.

Other than that occasional day off whose arrival I almost forgot (like Armistice Day) nothing was quite as exciting as the PTA Fun Night. It was a classic sort of school fair: at one end of the gym there were games of skill and chance (including a cakewalk!), and at the other, a buffet where you could get sloppy joes and potato chips on a paper plate. One of our teachers had dressed up like a Gypsy and offered to tell your fortune in the semi-darkened kindergarten room. No one worried that all the toy shelves along the windows compromised the air of mystery.

Other classrooms were allotted to all sorts of used stuff for sale: old clothing for sale in one, household items and bric-a-brac in another, and somewhere else, our absolute favorites: used comic books rolled up three to a bundle and sold for 5 cents apiece. When we got home, there was the magical moment: unrolling them out and seeing what we had gotten. There were always the losers like "Archie" or "Nancy," but more than a little excitement over some forbidden fruit like "True Detectives or "G.I. Joe." We always made sure we went through those items first, as it was more than likely the censor would turn up to inspect our haul.

During our childhood, there was a good deal less concern about children walking themselves to school. We had to cross a major street (Galena Boulevard, also US 30 and a major truck route) but there was no guard or other assistance. We were instructed to cross only at the corner with traffic lights but left to negotiate the rest of the trip on our own.

At the southwest corner of the school, there was a crossing guard to get children across either Walnut or Grand, neither of which was a busy street. It was manned by sixth graders who had passed muster for the "Student Patrol." It was a great matter of pride to put on the white canvas Sam Browne belt and command the younger kids. We were not allowed to stop traffic; our only duty was to assess when it was safe enough for people to cross. Still, I could hardly wait for my assigned week to come up and go on duty before and after school.

Schools were not much concerned about liability and litigation in those days. Nothing was more fun in winter than those times when the playground was blanketed with heavy snow. Our principal, Mr. Friday, a wise man in the psychology of youth, forbade the throwing of snowballs. He understood only too well that snowballs could be interpreted as a personal affront, and quickly turn into vendettas and reprisals. On the other hand, we were more than welcome to play group games in the snow, such as "King of the Mountain" on the large piles of snow that accumulated in the far corners of the playground. We also enjoyed a game called tackle tag. Tackle tag was played much like "Red Rover" though instead of getting tagged, you got tackled. Eventually, there would be only one or two survivors, usually the biggest and fastest sixth-grade boys. On snow days, everyone wanted to be early and get a game or two in before the bell. Our janitor astutely piled brooms at the entrances so that the excess snow could be brushed off before we came in.

While walking to school we had to pass the large Catholic elementary school. Our path, as dictated by our mother, required that we walk alongside their open playground. Relations between public school and Catholic students were not necessarily cordial. On several occasions, our small band was confronted by larger groups of adversaries who immediately launched into threats and jeers. As I look back, I suspect my fears of violence were exaggerated. The intent of our attackers was likely no more than intimidation or humiliation, though I confess on several occasions, I was apprehensive. But without fail, a defender would arrive to save the day. It was, of course, a nun—a fierce apparition in black and white who broke up the attack, smiled, and told us to get moving or we'd be late.

To this day, I have always been grateful to these women for saving my hide. And, I might add, the convent was famously generous on Halloween—even if the nuns knew you were a Protestant.

Sixth Grade at Todd, December 1955. I am the third boy from the right in the second row, partially hidden by the boy in front of me. Our mother is the woman in the lower left corner, back turned, wearing glasses and a hat. Just to my left is our teacher, Miss Faircloth, who was a great favorite with her students. Front row center, the boy with his hands in his pockets is Chip Brewick. Chip and I remained friends from first grade through high school graduation. Special thanks to Doug Scafe who provided this photograph.

The Quaker Five Year Meeting (1954)

The trip had an auspicious beginning,
excused from two days of school
and a four-hour ramble on the Pennsy,
en route to some unexplained event
being held at a small college deep in Indiana,
in part occasion for a small family reunion
and a homecoming of sorts for our mother.

The meetings themselves were deadly,
patches of silence without meaning,
followed by discussions I could not grasp,
but the communal meals were great fun,
a rump gathering of the Coggins clan,
where one of our uncles annoyed his sister
by teaching us a variety of spoon tricks.

Mother was delighted to meet old friends,
but we had to make do with cousins
who were not among our favorites.
In the end, blood and proximity trumped all,
an easy trade for our tired brown room
where all the books had been read
and the games played too many times.

Sunday morning finally arrived,
and as our mother made her farewells,
I wrote to a far distant father, duly reporting
that my younger brother was crabby,
eating an apple and reading the comics,
but had no words for a lost weekend,
the mysteries of adult pastimes—
but anxious for that train ride home.

Vacations

I don't think vacations were quite as common in the 1950s as they are today. One very important reason was the lack of discretionary income. The necessities of life (especially food and clothing) were then much more expensive, relatively speaking. Housing was perhaps less than today, but that was in part because people had much more modest expectations than in today's world of McMansions.

Travel itself was much different then. There was no Interstate system, which meant car trips were slow and tedious. Travel by train was not cheap, and air travel was somewhat of a luxury experience. Though we knew of the occasional brave souls who set out for Colorado or Florida in the family car, vacations tended to be less ambitious and less frequent. The visit to nearby family members or a week at a local campground was a staple of the "What I Did Last Summer" essay.

Our mother, though, was a lifelong travel enthusiast, and thanks to her rail heritage, a devotee of train trips. When a girl, her father took the family to Florida every winter. As a young woman, she journeyed all over the country, including Los Angeles, Chicago, and Philadelphia. Jon and I had the good fortune to be raised by a parent who thought travel was an essential part of life and enjoyed a number of interesting excursions while growing up.

I do not remember going anywhere until 1954 when we took two trips. The first was to Richmond, Indiana, in the spring to attend a Quaker Five Year Meeting. Nelle was anxious to see old friends from her active days in the church (she was not an active Friend in Aurora because there was no local meeting), but my brother and I were soon bored by all the various assemblies and events. Our high points in the trip were the first encounter with a Big Boy hamburger and the train rides to and from Chicago.

The next venture was much more interesting, a jaunt that summer back to Knoxville to visit with family and friends. Our Uncle Bill,

Nelle's younger brother, volunteered to come to Aurora and pick us up. We did not leave first thing in the morning and I recall being in Indianapolis in the middle of the night eating a White Castle burger and drinking orange soda. Mother tried to persuade Bill to take a break, but he demurred. We did not stop for the night and got to his home sometime the next day.

Tennessee, summer of 1954. Our mother and her
brother, Bill Coggins.

Bill and his wife Mary Lou were peripatetic. After several years of settled living in Oak Ridge (where he worked for Union Carbide, a prime contractor to Atomic Energy Commission), they never seemed to stay in any place for very long. At this point, they were renting an old farmhouse in the country outside Clinton, Tennessee. I remember following my two cousins, Larry and Allen, as we ran through the rows of corn in a nearby field, and to a stream where we could throw sticks in the water and watch them float away. Cousin Larry, older and more venturesome, tried to convince us to climb over a fence into a pasture with a bull, but we prudently declined. It was a novelty to be in a house with a TV, though Uncle Bill maintained close control over the viewing choices.

While there we made several trips into Knoxville, met old friends and family, and saw the old family homestead at 1720 Lombard Street. My brother and I marveled at the number of people Mother knew. While walking around downtown Knoxville she seemed to meet at least one person she knew on every block.

At the end of this visit, we got on the train and traveled to Wilmington, North Carolina, to visit some old friend of Mother's from Army days in WWII. I have no memories of the visit, but I do recall we had to change trains in Atlanta (even then you could not get anywhere in Dixie without going through Atlanta), and then get up at the crack of dawn to change trains once more. I was quite taken with the purple and gold livery of the coaches on the Atlantic Coast Line. After this interlude, we traveled on to Washington DC where we stayed with our mother's half-brother, Neil, who lived in Alexandria VA.

Washington was exciting. We spent every day going to the sights, including a tour at the FBI and the Treasury. There's nothing like machine guns and money to stimulate the imagination of a ten-year-old. Another high point was the Washington Monument. We took the elevator to the top, and our mother consented to let us walk down, though she declined to join us. I wanted to count the steps (898 according to my *Information Please Almanac*) but lost track within a few minutes and had to take the almanac on faith. We were also most thrilled with the boat ride down the Potomac to visit Mt. Vernon, and equally pleased with our souvenir tricorn hats, appropriately stitched with "Mt. Vernon." I can't remember going to either the White House or the Capitol. They would have been less interesting, anyway.

In 1956 we took a long spring vacation in California and stayed with Mother's cousin and aunt, who lived in La Puente just outside Los Angeles. We were among the first visitors to Disneyland, which had opened only a few months prior to our arrival and was still incomplete. In truth, both of us thought Knott's Berry Farm (an earlier theme park) was a lot more fun. We went home via San

Francisco and having only a free morning to tour before the train departed, our mother flagged a cab and told the driver to show us the sights, which he was happy to do. Then we had the excitement of being taken to our train (the California Zephyr, which left from Oakland) on a ferry. This trip featured a two-day train ride at either end, which got tiresome even for rail enthusiasts like the Bourgos, though on the Zephyr, my brother and I were much impressed with the club car where we enjoyed Cokes and the club sandwich.

California 1956. From left to right, Mike, Virginia Barnes, Jon and Larry Barnes. They were our second cousins.

The pattern of spring vacations continued. One year our mother took us to Detroit and contrary to her usual practice we took an airplane—our first airplane flight—and it may have been hers, too. Not only was it a thrill to be up in the air, but the airline served one of our favorites—roast beef and gravy—and for free. With the assistance of Gray Line Tours, we went to the Ford plant and visited the Old Greenfield Village. We were no doubt impressed by all the enterprise and ingenuity of Henry Ford's creations, but my brother's special memory was riding the wooden escalators at Hudson's department store (the ones at Field's were all metal). Before we went home, we crossed the border into Windsor, Ontario, our first visit outside the US (and possibly Mother's, too). We found Canada to be a little different (the candy was all English) but disappointingly, it was not at all exotic.

In addition to preferring spring travel, our mother was often inclined to make the trip an educational experience. Hence one year we traveled down to Hannibal, Missouri to see the Mark Twain attractions. One of the surviving photos of that trip shows me standing beside a historical marker dressed in a corduroy sports jacket, a reflection of how our parents thought we ought to look in public. Today, I suspect few boys of my age (I was 12 at the time) have ever worn a sports jacket—let alone worn one on vacation.

There I am, sports jacket and all, in 1957

The high (or low) point of this adventure was my brother coming down with some sort of 24-hour bug serious enough to alarm Nelle, so she asked the hotel to help her locate a doctor. Whatever the elderly doctor did to lose her confidence I do not recall, but it was immediately clear that she thought he was a quack. Jon did recover and we resumed our activities, including a visit to a cave (said to be the authentic location), where a guide tried to frighten the guests by turning off the lights without notice. Nelle was not pleased by this stunt and let him know so in no uncertain terms. Like all parents, she had a special gift for embarrassing her children in public.

As I got older, our father got into the vacation game, but given his travel schedule, it turned out the Christmas season was the easiest time of the year for him to join us. I recall two trips, once to Springfield (to see the Lincoln sites) and another to St. Louis. In each case, we rode the train to our destination and Dad decided we would travel first class in the parlor car, which was pretty much the cat's pajamas as far as we were concerned (our mother being more frugal, our trips with her—even the overnighters—were in coach). Each passenger got an individual swivel easy chair that could be reclined. We had the services of a classically attentive and efficient Pullman porter. It was the day of the named trains and we rode the *Abraham Lincoln* and the *Ann Rutledge* on the Gulf, Mobile & Ohio line.

Once again, the services of the Gray Line were summoned to furnish us with a peek at all that mattered. Al and Nelle always believed in farming out the tourism to the experts rather than arming themselves with brochures and guiding themselves through the sights. All this was fine with me: the confident and knowledgeable style of the guides always assured me I was in the hands of an expert. Our vacations were almost always urban. Neither of our parents cared for the outdoors and they always enjoyed staying in hotels, which in that day meant the classic pile downtown. Somewhere along the line, they introduced us to room service. My brother and I could not quite believe the elaborate ritual the room service waiter went through as he set the table and retrieved all the food from the warming compartments below.

One of the shorter trips was a Burlington rail tour to Prairie du Chien, Wisconsin, (a day trip) where we visited The Effigy Mounds National Monument. I have regrettably lost a snapshot of my brother (then about eight) wearing his motorcycle cap a la Marlon Brando—an early augury of his later dashing ways. Late in the day, we had supper at a local restaurant. Some forty years later, my wife and I built a second home in the country north of Prairie, and soon discovered Kaber's, an old restaurant downtown near the tracks. I immediately realized it was the place where we had had supper on our tour those many years back. As is often the case in small town America, not much had changed in the intervening years.

The last family trip with Mother was another Burlington rail tour, but one that took us to Colorado Springs, where we visited Pike's Peak, the Garden of the Gods, and the last night, had dinner and a show at a dude ranch. The meal was undistinguished and produced complaints from many of our fellow diners. Thinking it was authentic chuck wagon fare, Jon and I had no objections. Whatever temptation we might have had to think that the fellows walking around were real cowboys soon disappeared. Roy Rogers notwithstanding, we knew Randolph Scott would have never stooped to singing and telling jokes for the tourists.

California (1956)

That April we boarded the El Capitan,
forty hours of plains, mountains, and desert
across eight states from Chicago to Los Angeles,
a long day of comic books and card games,
a glimpse of real Indians at Albuquerque,
finally leaving the train at Pasadena
where the California cousins awaited us.

We hiked in the desert at Twenty-nine Palms,
visited the new Disneyland and Olvera Street,
and watched a bank robbery at Knott's,
chauffeured through this wonderland
by cousin Marjorie's one-eyed husband,
who would turn to talk to the back seat,
leaving his glass eye to watch the road.

I fell in love with my cousin Virginia,
a nine-year-old beauty who took no notice,
and excessively admired her brother,
a boy who was everything I was not.
Slim, expert and confident,
he helped his father kill the chickens
destined for the Sunday dinner menu.

Heading back we stopped in San Francisco,
where my brother's delicate constitution
recoiled at the fishy smells of Joe DiMaggio's,
leaving us to pot roast and peas at the hotel.
After a night and a cruise across the bay,
two days on the Zephyr got us home by noon
and to the cruelest of betrayals—
school for the rest of the day.

The Joys of Being Raised by Eccentric Parents

I have recently read several memoirs of childhood back in the 1950s and 60s. The writers typically place much emphasis on how utterly conventional their parents were back then. However, ours were not.

To start, our parents were widely separated by age, but not in the "normal" manner. Our mother was eleven years older than our father. The family tale is that she was a confirmed old maid until he arrived and persuaded her to change her mind. They were 36 and 25, respectively, when they got married in 1940, and from all evidence, it was a match that worked out to their mutual satisfaction. Both were entirely capable of ignoring the opinions of others when it suited them, and they never worried in the least over the matter. It was an unusual union in that day and age, for though the conformity of the 1950s is sometimes exaggerated, it was a time when people did tend to hew to the norms.

They were also a varied combination of geography and background. Dad was from Joliet, Illinois, and mostly descended from recent Catholic immigrants. Mother was from Knoxville, Tennessee, a Quaker, and from a family that had been in the United States for a long time, but only recently emerged from Appalachia. Once again, such a twain made no difference. Both made compromises (she more than he) but neither ever strayed far from his or her origins. Nelle was always the proud Southerner, and as he aged, Dad inched closer and closer back to his Catholic roots.

Our parents also had opinions that placed them outside the mainstream of Aurora, Illinois. My brother and I were not exhorted to be pious (though we were regulars at church and said grace at meals). Such staples as family prayer or Bible reading, common among Protestants in the 1950s, were unknown in our home. Nor were we particularly patriotic, though we certainly celebrated the national holidays and our mother was an active political participant. Al and Nelle thought religious fervor and pride in one's country were virtues best enjoyed privately.

Thus, neither one of us grew up with any fear of hell, nor were we likely to be crushed at some future date when it became apparent the USA was not entirely perfect. Likewise, our parents did not join in the national hysteria over the possibility of nuclear war. Though they made no effort to shield us from the news, such a catastrophe was never a major item of discussion in our home. Both of us had classmates whose parents managed to scare their children half to death over the prospects of atomic war.

Our father had a detached and skeptical view of the political scene. His heroes were FDR and his chief from apprentice days at the TVA, David Lilienthal—people who knew how to get stuff done. Pontificators like John Foster Dulles drove him crazy and he genuinely loathed Joseph McCarthy. He was one of the few people in that time who understood that the Cold War, though not a trivial threat, also operated to the benefit of both sides in their domestic political agendas. To my knowledge, though, he never voted in a national election, though in later years my mother talked him into registering so that he could vote in school elections.

Mother was a dyed-in-the-wool Democrat, and one of those rare souls, a Southern liberal. Racial segregation and discrimination offended her, and even in Illinois in 1951 her feelings were not typical of the white population. Finding Aurora to be hopelessly Republican, she turned her energy to the PTA and school elections, where she soon was a force in electing school board members.

There were several aspects of life with Al and Nelle that were not so comfortable for their offspring. We never owned a car, not so much an issue when we were young, but once in high school, it was a definite limitation to one's social life. One never knew how that girl might react to being picked up in a taxi for a trip to the movies. If we had lived in New York, all well and good—but this was in Aurora, Illinois, where one of the badges of young manhood was a set of car keys.

I was also keenly aware that I dressed in a manner different from my peers. Mother never approved of blue jeans except for summer or weekend wear. As Dad moved up the ladder at the firm, he determined he wanted his sons to be properly outfitted (no doubt as he would have wished in his youth). In time, then, all our clothes came from nice outfits in Chicago, and I, at least, always had the fear that I was advertising a certain sartorial superiority—which in the world of youthful conformity is the last thing one wishes to do.

Other details troubled us. There was the question of our father's prolonged absences while he worked overseas. After all, most fathers were home every night for dinner. Other kids did not have to go through scout meetings, confirmation, even high school graduation without Dad on hand. Our mother's Southern background sometimes came through and she tended (as an older parent and one from a culturally more conservative region) to enforce a somewhat old-fashioned code of behavior.

The clothing issue was much in keeping with their outlook on life, which was always very much their own. They briefly owned one house, and never bought another. We lived in a series of rented houses, all of which were rather modest in size, neighborhood location, and amenities, but Nelle and Al enjoyed filling them with beautiful furniture. Both enjoyed good quality in clothing, eating out on a regular basis, and vacationing in nice hotels. Mother loved to travel and took us on many interesting trips. Dad acquired an enormous library of books, many of which still sit on our shelves. They were zealous in making sure we had profitable summer experiences starting with camps and ending with foreign language summer school. Few of our peers, even those whose parents had similar (or greater) resources, were given such opportunities.

So, we were aware that other kids found our parents a little odd and our lives a little different. I am not sure either of them paid quite enough attention to the issue of how their children managed to fit into the world around them; as eccentrics and independents, it was of no great importance to them. Likewise, children can be the worst judges of their parents' lives. Then as now, children can be quite unfair in insisting that their parents not disturb the boundaries of social comfort in the slightest way.

It is the American habit to look to the bottom line, and what we find there is revealing. Both my brother and I have been distressingly functional adults. Neither of us picked up the ambition bug to the degree our father had it, but both of us have largely accomplished what we set out to do. The essential message we got at the hearth when growing up was to do what was right, to be kind and considerate to others, and to finish the job. We were counseled not to be overly consumed with ourselves, and to remember that grand crusades are rare—but each day needs to be put to good use. Any sort of racial, religious or ethnic bias is the mark of an ignorant soul, and a gentleman always stands up when another person enters the room.

We Never Had a Car

I am sure this chapter will seem improbable to anyone of my generation. Today, interest in owning a car is finally on the decline, especially among younger people. It was quite the contrary in the 1950s when I was growing up. Most every family I knew had one, though the two-car norm was some years in the future.

We did not own a car. I am not sure Alfred Bourgo ever drove one, though I know my grandfather owned an automobile. There is a photo of him standing beside a substantial sedan from 1935 or so. Our mother drove for a while in the early 1930s when she was doing social work for American Friends Service in eastern Kentucky. Her story was that she was never a confident driver and was happy to give it up. I can't imagine the roads in that place and era would have done much to make driving an enjoyable experience.

Why did our parents refuse to own a car? I have never known the exact reasons, but I think the answer may be quite simple: they did not want to be bothered with the business of ownership. Our father was overseas at his job sites anywhere from 6 to 9 months a year. Given Nelle's refusal to resume driving, the car would have been idle much of the year. This continued until 1968 when my brother was 20. That year he bought a car and became the family chauffeur for several years.

So how did we get around? In the early 1950s, it was a lot easier to live without a car than it is now, even in a small city like Aurora, Illinois. There was a municipal bus service that covered a good deal of the town (it was before the days of suburban sprawl) and ran at fifteen-minute intervals. The fare was a dime for adults and a nickel for children. It was easy to take the bus to the large public park on the other side of town, the hospital, shopping, and other places of interest.

The other feature of life that made it easy to get around was that there were not yet any shopping centers. Downtown was still the place you went to conduct the business of daily life. If you lived close to downtown, as we did for the first eight years in Aurora, then all it took was a brief bus ride or a fifteen-minute walk and you had almost everything downtown Aurora had to offer inside a compact area of twelve square blocks or so.

We may have never had a car, but Uncle Hugh and Aunt Betty were always equipped. This picture is from a visit they made to Knoxville in 1948 when Betty talked me into posing with her baby Tenna's sunbonnet on.

Walking was the order of the day in that era. Schools were oriented to a small geography and almost every student walked or rode a bicycle to school. My brother and I walked to the movies, the library, the YMCA and even down to the railroad station (almost a mile) when we wanted to see one of the Burlington Zephyrs roll into the station. When we went to the movies, our mother provided bus fare, but we often chose to spend our nickels on a candy bar instead of a ride home.

One of the benefits of walking is learning the landscape in detail. My brother and I explored downtown Aurora on our own starting from the ages of about 9 and 6, respectively, the point at which Mother decided we could navigate the route on our own. We soon knew the name of every street and every store, and every so often there was the pleasure of finding a new business or a wistful parting with an old familiar that had shuttered.

Downtown was a form of entertainment. If there was nothing else to do, then why not head down the hill and check out the store windows? The variety of visual display ranged from the immaculately laid out scenes at Block and Kuhl's (a local department store), which changed frequently, to the windows at the Greek candy store, which looked like they hadn't been changed in eons. We would wander up one street and down another, equally delighted in the novel and the familiar, and without a nickel to our names. We were consumers—but in our own fashion.

When it was time to head home we had to decide which route to choose. One was the shortest and most direct if we were in a hurry, a second offered the treat of being able to see the Fox river spilling over the dam, and the third offered the thrill of wandering up Benton past the *Beacon News* building and then through a neighborhood with the slightly menacing aspect of buildings in decay.

In fall 1954, when I was in the 5th grade, things began to change. We left the apartment and moved to a spacious Victorian four square a block away. New furniture appeared, we started eating out more often, and soon, and our clothes were no longer purchased in Aurora but from stores in Chicago. Our father had passed some milestone at the office and suddenly, we were much more prosperous. There was soon a change in our mode of transportation.

We now entered what I will call the cab era, in which taxis became our parents' principal mode of transportation. When Dad was in residence, he took them to and from the Burlington station, where he commuted to Chicago. Our mother could now take advantage of certain shopping opportunities not possible by bus, such as the first shopping center in Aurora, which opened about 1957. We started exploring more distant restaurants like the Bit o' Sweden or the Highway Lounge. As time went on, she got deeper and deeper into her various volunteer and political activities, and dinner was more frequently eaten at restaurants with a cab ride at both ends of the evening.

Our parents were oriented to brand loyalty. They believed in finding a reliable source and sticking with it. As far as they were concerned the extra service and consideration that should come from a loyal relationship more than offset any cost saving to be earned by shopping around. They soon settled on Yellow Cab (one of the three outfits in town) and we soon had a whole bunch of new acquaintances who hauled us around town. Al and Nelle's belief in the power of tipping made us desirable customers and we rarely had to wait long for someone to show up.

There was Paul, a thin wiry, little fellow who looked like he could have been cast as a labor organizer in *On the Waterfront.* Paul was a proud working man, but he never made us feel too uncomfortable in our bourgeois skins. Fittingly enough, when it was time for me to start Knox College in the fall of 1962, Paul was duly engaged as my personal chauffeur and drove me to Galesburg (though in his own car, not a taxi). He was pleased to have a role in my new venture and did not make me self-conscious about being there—at what was a relatively expensive private college.

Next, I remember Ernie, a gruff but friendly Kentuckian who liked to discuss Southern cuisine with our mother. He also went to college with me as Paul's companion and relief driver. (Unlike Paul, he was generous with his thoughts about going to college.) There were others whose names I cannot recall but whose particular details are still with me. One driver had only one hand but managed the wheel and the manual shift in the Checker Marathon taxi with no apparent sweat.

Another was a veteran of the Flying Tigers in WWII, who loaned me some of his personal photographs taken at the base in China where he served. (Somehow, they were never returned, and regretfully, I still have them). There was a fellow whose sons were deeply involved in Scouting (as was I) and fittingly enough, one

Friday night he drove me out to the local campsite when my promised ride to the weekend event fell through.

My brother and I encountered various baseball fans among the drivers, but none of them shared our love for the White Sox. We often chafed at their dismissal of Our Team, but we knew that being a Sox fan was a lonely calling in Aurora, and as good children of that era we did not contradict adults, even when they were dumb enough to cheer for the Cubs.

The Pleasures of Downtown

It is hard to exaggerate how much my brother and I enjoyed going downtown. There were always crowds and it felt like a carnival where you never knew quite what you might see. In the days when local retail predominated, every store had its own individual atmosphere—some neat, some untidy—some colorful, some drab— some friendly, some gruff—unlike today's world of national retailers with their uniform layouts, strategies, and styles.

Downtown was a place where all sorts of human beings interacted. In a place as large as Aurora (population 51,000 in those days) life was not pristine, and on occasion, we encountered someone or something Mother felt no need to explain, especially if we were near North Broadway where things started to get seedy. (Such episodes were how we learned one of childhood's most important lessons— when to recognize that any further questions to the parent will be counterproductive.)

An example of the best downtown had to offer was the Woolworth dime store. It operated on the same economic model as today's dollar stores, but little else was comparable. A Woolworth's was clean, well-ordered, and predictably stocked. Unlike the stores of today, the sales floor was not divided into aisles separated by shelves, but a large collection of square or rectangular counters, a collection of islands across the floor, each containing its own category of stuff—housewares, toys, clothing, and so forth. As you came in the front door, the whole store lay before your eyes.

Merchandise was neatly laid out on these counters in various compartments, often separated by glass dividers. Inside each counter unit was an open well area where a clerk might stand to assist customers. These were often older people who paid close attention to small boys looking through the bins of cars and trucks, airplanes, toy soldiers, cowboys and Indians, and the like. The price points were just right: even if we only had ten cents, we might find something desirable we could afford.

Woolworth's also had two other features that stood out. First, there was a pet department which featured birds (canaries and parakeets) in cages. There were rows and rows of tanks with goldfish, angelfish and all the like. The birds could be heard throughout the store and we always gave this area a careful perusal, though we knew better than to ask our mother to invest in one of these critters. (A Woolworth's always had a lunch counter somewhere in the store, which by today's standards is rather suspect—food service in the same area as live birds. Things were more relaxed in that earlier age. My memory is we rarely if ever ate there.)

The other big draw was near the front window: a machine which made doughnuts before our very eyes! This marvelous device had a conveyor in the bottom of the machine, something along the lines of a carousel made of separate metal squares floating and turning in hot grease. Some mechanism would drop a circle of raw dough into each empty square as it passed. At the halfway point into its circular journey, another engineering wonder would flip the donut and the uncooked side got its turn to brown. After 360 degrees, another lever flipped it into a bin of powdered sugar where it was retrieved by a store employee and set in a display case. Knowing Mother's feelings about the rights and wrongs of food (and she was as confident in these attitudes as she was about birds), we knew better than to ask for one of these, too.

Other stops were of less interest. New clothes did not excite us much, we found the local department store to be a bore, and the visit to Somebody's Dry Goods seemed to last forever. We had far more fun on expeditions without a parent.

There remained the question of finance. A trip downtown was much enhanced by the prospect of being able to purchase something. Sadly, our parents were not profligate on money matters. We did get modest allowances in exchange for doing a few chores like taking out the trash and we could return the pop bottles for the deposit. If each boy had a six pack in each hand, that brought in a whole forty-eight cents, more than enough to fund a worthwhile experience. So, our ventures into the world of commerce (on days when bottles were available) included visiting the Jewel Tea, a grocery store where we could redeem the bottles and conveniently located on our route.

One of our favorite stops was Aurora Stamp and Coin, operated by two retired postal workers and located in the dusty upstairs of an old office building. There never were many customers, and one of the two owners was almost always willing to spend time going through stamps for sale with two boys who rarely had more than fifty cents apiece to spend on new acquisitions. All purchases were carefully inserted into translucent envelopes, and we left feeling we had completed a significant transaction and eager to get home and fill in that empty space in the album.

We were also well known at the Book Shop, not so much as clients but as the children of regular customers. In our early years, we would have never had enough money to buy a book on our own, but the owners, Mr. and Mrs. Kohn, were happy to allow us to browse at leisure while rewarding us with conversation and attention. No doubt, they recognized the importance of priming us with ideas we might pass on to a parent. We appreciated being treated as customers and not just mere children.

A few years later, when teenagers and confirmed book lovers with a few bucks to spend, we would have never considered going anywhere else for a book. My library has much changed over the past fifty years, but I am pleased I still have a few titles I bought in that store.

Some places we went just to say hello. The lady who ran the Hallmark store was a neighbor, an older woman we thought exotic and glamorous, and always happy to see us. We might also pause at Newman's Pharmacy, where the owner would greet us and let us linger over his excellent selection of comic books. If we did have the requisite dime, the choice was exceedingly difficult, though narrowed by our mother's rules, which were well understood. Bugs Bunny, Uncle Scrooge, and the Lone Ranger were acceptable. GI Joe and Police Stories were not. Superman and Batman were not encouraged, but acceptable (though in truth neither of us much cared for superheroes).

Wandering up and down the streets brought its own rewards. There was always the policeman on his motor tricycle looking for parking violators, and once in a while, the excitement of a ticket being inserted under a wiper. Passing the movie theaters, you could see what was coming next, valuable information to have, and especially near Christmas, when mysteriously, as the day grew closer, our parents might want to have us out of the house for a few hours. Or we could stare into the dark spaces behind the windows of a bar, getting that unmistakable whiff of stale beer if some sinner happened to be coming or going.

But sooner or later, the magic began to wear down. Even small boys get tired. We had been citizens of our town—done the tour, spent our money, or the clock at the bank might be pointing to a time close to the appointed hour. It was time to walk home and think of something else to do.

The Magic of Memory

Are these lovely thoughts a memory,
or just thoughts posing as one?
Memory is perhaps a traitor,
but my age, it is a kindly one
when it brings a summer afternoon,
moments of sixty years ago:
my brother and I emerged from the movies,
blinking as we re-entered that sunny day.

We headed for home but with careful haste,
lingering along shop windows and then lawns:
dutiful, no doubt, but in no hurry.
Waiting at home was trash to take out,
orders to take a bath and put on clean clothes,
but for now, we could talk about cowboys,
our favorite baseball players,
or castles, knights and other fancies.

To revisit a time when time meant nothing,
because there seemed so much of it,
to return briefly to a happy day
swelled by memory's careless generosity—
for such a gift, there is only gratitude:
veracity is a noble thing, to be prized,
but thankfully, we do not live under oath,
and sometimes, verisimilitude will suffice.

What We Read

Thanks to Mother and Dad, Jon and I were active readers from an early age. Books were simply an accepted part of life as we knew it. Mother was an enthusiastic reader, though her tastes (mostly light fiction) were less ambitious than our father's, who enjoyed serious fiction, history, and biographies. They read to us, encouraged us to read, and books were a regular gift item. Nelle and Al resisted the TV bandwagon for a long time and I was 12 before we had a TV in the house. Thus, for quite a while we relied on books for a substantial portion of our entertainment.

In early years our parents took me through A.A. Milne (Winnie the Pooh) Beatrice Potter (Peter Rabbit), *The Wizard of Oz* and fairy tales. Dad enjoyed old fashioned narrative poetry and read us "The Highwayman," "The Inchcape Rock," and "The boy stood on the burning deck…" I was a precocious reader and soon discovered the charms of the newspaper and almanacs. One of the first serious books I remember reading was *A Child's History of the World.* The chapters on the Egyptians with all their mummies and the Assyrians with all their plundering were a little frightening and hard to shake when trying to fall asleep.

School was another part of the equation. Each classroom at Mary A. Todd School had its own small library where we could select books for the free reading period each day. In the second or third grade, both my brother I found our favorites on that shelf to be a series of books called *The Childhoods of Famous Americans*. There were, for example, *George Washington, Boy Leader*, *Ben Franklin, Boy Printer,* or *Abigail Adams, Girl of Colonial America*. Each book followed the same format. The bulk of the text was about the childhood of the subject character. A final chapter provided an epilogue that sketched the adult accomplishments of our hero or heroine.

I recently learned this series has been around for a long time. It was already in existence in the 1940s and new titles have been added even in recent years. No doubt, these were fictionalized biographies. There was considerable dialogue provided and a level of detail that suggested imagination was in play. It never occurred to us to worry about how the author knew exactly what George Washington had bravely said to the neighborhood bully on a specific day in October 1743. Or how the writer learned the exact words George Washington Carver uttered on the day he decided to dedicate his life to plant science. As far as we were concerned, we were getting the straight scoop.

But no matter: we enjoyed the stories, developed an enthusiasm for history and managed to learn a few facts about the chief characters of our American saga. Most of the heroes were white males, but surprisingly enough for that day, women and minorities were not entirely ignored. Susan B. Anthony, Booker Washington, and Sequoyah all got included.

I was not much interested in juvenile fiction, and for that reason, there are a lot of classics I never read—for example, *Charlotte's Web*. If I read fiction it was more likely to be genre fiction, and my favorites were baseball and science fiction. On trips to the library, I was always game for another entry in the Blue Sox series by Duane Decker (a total of 12 were published from 1947 to 1964) or anything that resembled a good space opera. It never occurred to me that most of the science fiction I read differed from Westerns only in the mode of conveyance used to get around. My brother's tastes ran in different directions. He was a big fan of Tom Swift and the Hardy Boys. Though he shared my love for baseball stories, his favorite sports author was John R. Tunis.

The public library was a favorite outing. It was in a classic Carnegie building on the south edge of downtown, easily accessible on foot or by bus, and could have served as the stereotype of the old-fashioned library. A staff of helpful and efficient women enforced the rule of silence. Checking a book out (one was allowed only a few at a time) brought on the wonderful rituals of cards being shuffled and a rubber stamp attached to end of a pencil applying dates in red ink.

There was nothing quite like the day when we were finally old enough to have our own library cards. It was a true rite of passage into maturity and standing. During the summer there were programs designed to lure children into reading with small tokens or certificates offered as a reward. I still have my "Space Cadets" certificate from 1952, which attests that I read eight books "suitable to the student's grade level" that summer. To get credit you had to be interviewed by the children's librarian on each book you claimed. I was nervous each time I approached her desk to get my next star.

Having cut our teeth on famous childhoods, we moved on in later years to the "Landmark" series, which was another series of books, mostly American history. Some of the books were about individual events like the battle of Gettysburg. Others like the *Story of the Foreign Legion* covered a topic. A little research has confirmed my recollection that these were well written and accurate accounts (I was highly disappointed to learn the greatest dangers faced by American troops in the Spanish American War were tropical disease, tainted rations, and gross incompetence in the supply corps—not heroic efforts.) Many of these books were by well-known writers and journalists and some were adaptations of adult titles.

I also liked mythology, especially Greek and Roman, and practically wore out *Myths and Classic Tales*. Robin Hood was another favorite, and the flyleaf of my copy of *Robin Hood and His Merry Outlaws* by J. Walker McSpadden (1923) duly notes I had read it at least three times between 1953 and 1956. (I also crossed out my name as written by our mother and wrote it myself). The *Wizard of Oz* was another volume I enjoyed numerous times, though the number is not similarly documented. (I happily confess I recently re-read it, to great enjoyment.)

The Grimm's Fairy Tales in the Scribner Classics edition got a lot of my attention. I was highly aware this rendition was the real thing and far from the bowdlerized versions we encountered in more polite books or the Disney films. (When I read some of these a few years ago with a nine-year-old grandson he was just as fascinated as

I had been with the raw view of life in these tellings.) We had a lovely collection of the Scribner volumes, including books by Walter Scott, Stevenson, and most had the celebrated illustrations by N.C. Wyeth.

Robin Hood was a perfect illustration of our reading strategy. If you couldn't lay your hands on something new that seemed interesting, then why not give one of the old favorites another spin? I can't recall how many times I read *The Story of the Foreign Legion*, but the book never failed to deliver the goods. My heart always started to beat a little faster when the last six Legionnaires, surrounded and out of ammunition, fixed bayonets and charged 2,000 enemy troops at the battle of Camarón in 1863. Afterward, their adversary was gracious enough to allow the three remaining survivors to return to their lines as the escort for the body of their heroic leader Capitaine Danjou. That was the sort of gallantry you could talk about for an entire afternoon without losing an ounce of wonder and admiration.

Shoes, Food, and Other Miscellany

In the 50s shoes were a much different matter than today. These days, most shoes come in two widths, and aside from a few upscale places, shopping for shoes is a self-service operation. Back then, buying shoes was done with the assistance of an expert sales person who measured feet with various and sundry precision instruments to make sure one got the perfect fit. Shoes came in an elaborate variety of widths starting with "A" (very narrow) and ranging out to EEEE (called "duck feet" by our father). Although a few of the department stores had shoe sections, the specialty shoe store still reigned supreme—unlike today, when the only survivors are either luxury outlets or places that sell running shoes, work shoes, etc.

Shoes were expensive, relatively speaking, in 1955. A $10 pair of shoes for children cost the equivalent of $90 in 2017, and few people today routinely spend that kind of money on shoes for their offspring. These were shoes that could be repaired, and visits to the shoe repair store for new soles and heels were a regular activity.

Our mother was most attentive to our shoes. We presented her with multiple worries in the foot department and she was determined to find the best solutions. I was early diagnosed with flat feet and horrors—put my weight on the outside of my feet. Today, no one gets terribly excited about flat feet, but back then it was thought to be a serious issue and was even cause for deferment from the military draft. Thus, in her mind it was essential I have shoes with arch support and a reinforced heel. My brother had extremely wide feet, which meant ordinary shoe stores were often unable to supply his EEEE size.

Buying shoes became quite an event. Aurora had no outlet that would meet our needs. The nearest was in LaGrange, a suburb about 25 miles away, but luckily, on the rail line into Chicago, and conveniently near the train station. So, several times a year we would go on a shoe expedition to LaGrange. It also included a stop for lunch at a restaurant in downtown LaGrange where we first encountered waffle fries, both exotic and sophisticated fare.

Shoes were used on a cycle. Before school, we got two new pairs of shoes—one dress (reserved for church and special occasions) and a pair of high-top tennis shoes for recess and gym at school. The last pair of leather shoes was used for everyday wear such as school until it no longer fit. When school ended, our "gym" shoes became our everyday wear in the summer, and by the end of the summer, they were pretty much in tatters. Like most children, we were tough on our shoes. When our father managed to get home after one of his sojourns in the Middle East, one of his first remarks was that our shoes were terribly scuffed, and thus, one of his first chores was to get out the polishing kit and restore his sons' footwear to a gentlemanly shine.

It is hard to think about the past without thinking about food. We were both crazy about the taste of chocolate malt and we would consume it in any number of ways. Our favorite was a chocolate malted milk made with ice cream, but that was available only when eating out. At home, we had to rely on chocolate malt powder that never dissolved very well in cold milk. There were also Horlick's malted milk tablets, marketed as a health food in drug stores, but that we thought of as candy in a roll.

Some food items were popular in part thanks to their packaging. Wizard of Oz peanut butter came in jars designed to be used as a glass when the contents were consumed. Kraft cheese jars were saved when empty for breakfast juice glasses. Spam and Vienna sausage were great fun because one opened the can with the key attached to the bottom and not a can opener. It was always a challenge to see if you could roll up the tear strip in one smooth circle. We liked the contents, too—and both of us still enjoy them many years later, to the horror of our respective wives.

Some of the staples in our diet would cause equal horror among health-conscious parents. Such items as condensed soups, Chef Boyardee pasta, pork and beans, and Dinty Moore beef stew were favorite items, mostly for lunch. Nelle was an industrious cook when it came to dinner, especially if the old man was around, but at noontime, she was inclined to convenience. All these food items shared numerous important qualities: lots of sodium, preservatives, fats and many were made by the Campbell (which she always pronounced as "camel") Soup Company. I was also a great fan of the unspeakable lunch meats of the time (talk about mystery meat), but my brother was allergic to nitrites or one of the other preservatives and could not tolerate hot dogs, baloney and the like.

Our taste in cheese was likewise primitive. The closest we saw of a decent cheese by today's thinking was cheddar, sold in blocks and referred to as "rat cheese." Cheese also included such delicacies as cottage cheese, cream cheese and best of all, Kraft Velveeta Cheese, which was the magic ingredient in any number of casseroles and conglomerations. Jon and I did not care for rat cheese, but we thought Velveeta was delicious. One would think suspicion should have been raised by the fact that Velveeta did not have to be refrigerated.

Our food choices at the grocery store were much different in those days. Today, there must be at least six varieties of Cheerios cereal or Hellman's mayonnaise. I read recently that one of the popular pasta sauces now offers twenty-eight different varieties. To do so the food makers have cut back on the sizing options. Many products are offered in one size—jumbo. By contrast in the 1950s, most products were offered in one variety and in a choice of smaller quantities or sizes—in part a reflection of the fact that we all lived in much smaller spaces in those days and on tighter budgets.

We were on hand for the launch of another food product often blamed for just about every ill in the country short of the national debt. That would be pre-sweetened cereals, which first appeared nation-wide in 1949, but I don't recall having them until I was about eight. Sugar Crisp, Sugar Pops, and Sugar Frosted Flakes were all early favorites, though my brother and I never lost our taste for the original versions of Cheerios, Rice Crispies, and Kix. Another infamous food that turned up in these years was the TV dinner, the first in wave after wave of prepared meals sold frozen. One issue in their introduction was that many homes still had a tiny freezer compartment that could not accommodate much more than ice trays, a few boxes of frozen vegetables and a can of condensed orange juice. I can't remember the first refrigerator we had with a more spacious freezer, but it would have not been much before 1956.

In the early years in Aurora, food was still marketed door to door—in our case by the Jewel Tea man, who dropped in every few weeks. He would carry a sample case, conveniently loaded with items we had purchased in the past, plus whatever else he thought might get Nelle's attention. My brother and I always hovered around to see what treats might be forthcoming, especially at Christmas times when he brought frosted cookies covered with seasonal sprinkles.

Like many people who served us then, the Jewel Tea man wore a uniform. Uniforms were the order of the day—the milkman, nurses, pharmacists, the various delivery men, the guy from the dry cleaners, the mail carrier, bus drivers, train conductors, school crossing guards, and even gas station attendants. It was a more formal age—male clerks in stores invariably wore a suit and tie and the women employees were always in skirts. The owner of our local neighborhood grocery was invariably seen in a white jacket with a dress shirt and bow tie. The fellow who fixed our shoes wore a tie, which could not have been very handy around some of the equipment he used. Ties are always a temptation for machines with moving parts.

 Formal dress extended throughout daily life. Office workers were expected to work in jackets and ties. People dressed up to go out to supper (even if they were just going to the local hash house) and for shopping, movies, and travel. Even little boys were expected to put on the monkey suit for such occasions as church, holiday meals, and certain formal visits. Children today will never know how much fun it was to wear a freshly starched shirt with the collar buttoned tight.

This morning I was looking at some old photos, and lo and behold—I found my brother at age four in his gray flannels and sporting a natty bow tie. Then as now, the man had a feeling for his haberdashery. I have always been jealous of his sense of style.

Mother and sons about 1953. Those lapel pins were received for dutiful attendance at Sunday school. It appears there must have been a recent trip to the barber shop.

Hobbies, Games and the YMCA

In emulation of our parents, both Jon and I pursued a variety of hobbies when we were kids. Both of us were early to take up stamp collecting. We learned the basics from Dad, who showed us how to soak stamps off envelopes and mount them in our albums with hinges. We quickly learned Scott's Publishing was the gold standard of the trade. They issued the catalogs we used as an aid in our efforts to get our stamps pasted onto the album page that matched the country they were from. This was not always an easy thing to manage at the age of seven or eight. Why, for example, did the Hungarians insist on calling their country *Magyarorszag*? Or what about the Finns: what did *Suomi* mean? Even Germany called itself by a strange name. It was even worse when you had to deal with a country that used the Cyrillic alphabet, and almost hopeless as you migrated into Asia.

But sooner or later we started to figure all this out. The Scotts album had plenty of the stamps illustrated on the pages, which was a great help. Our father also loaned us the Scott's *Stamp Identifier*, a handy pamphlet that led us through the mysteries of distinguishing Siam from Outer Mongolia. Since we were still living in the twilight years of the British Empire, many countries and territories helpfully printed their stamps in English.

Getting new stamps was a major goal for us. In the early years, we went for quantity, buying packets labeled "500 International Stamps—Guaranteed All Different." (No surprise: they weren't.) We would contend over the right to go through the mail each day to see if there were any new issues that we didn't have. Those were the days before metered mail started interfering with the use of real stamps. Since Harza Engineering did a lot of business overseas and it was long before the day of faxes and e-mails, they received a fair amount of mail from overseas. Dad might bring home envelopes with all sorts of exotic postage stamps. When he came home from one of his trips abroad, he would sometimes pass out mint stamps (very exciting, as almost all our stamps were used) from places like Iraq and Jordan.

Later, we started getting more selective and concentrated on trying to build specific collections, particularly of US stamps. For this, we would visit our friend at Aurora Stamp and Coin whenever we had a few dollars to spend. It quite satisfying to peruse all those pages in the album filled with complete issues—not a blank spot on the page—but I never lost my taste for going through those mixed packets, traveling in my mind from Argentina and Andorra to Ceylon and Czechoslovakia. There was nothing like looking through the pages of the album itself and encountering such names as Memel, the Ionian Islands and Wurttemberg—now vanished from the atlas—but places where people once went to the post office, bought stamps bearing those names and put them on envelopes.

At various times my brother and I also essayed coin collecting (one of our mother's interests), but for me, it was not a successful hobby. As was often remarked of me when young, I was not a good saver.

Speaking of hobbies, our mother's Hummel figurines can be seen in the bookcase to the left. As for the bookcase itself, I am looking at it as I write this since it sits on my desk. The desk caddy on the top can be seen in my brother's home. I can't determine what Jon and I are holding.

I can still hear our mother clucking as she made sharp (but accurate) observations about my profligate ways. In short, my collection failed to prosper because I had an unfortunate tendency to treat the coins I had saved for my collection as a piggy bank to be raided. My brother was far more disciplined and was often held up as an example I ought to follow in matters financial.

Various other pursuits occupied me from time to time. Mother got me started on postcards by giving me a collection she had puttered with, and for a time I added items to the collection, but my interest did not last. I was an enthusiastic devotee of plastic models, particularly the aircraft of World War II, but my results were sloppy, and I would have never dreamed of tackling anything as challenging as our father did. Unlike the rest of my hobbies, which all faded at some point or the other, bird identification has been a lifelong interest and I still get excited when I spot some confusing spring warbler early in May.

Playing games was something we both enjoyed. Starting with the Uncle Wiggly Game, my brother and I got hooked on board games. Then as now, Monopoly was a very popular game, though our elders always resisted playing with us because they felt it took too long. We had better luck getting them to play Parcheesi and Sorry, which required briefer time spans. In 1955 Parker Brothers issued a new game called "Careers." Jon and I were immediate fans of this game and played it endlessly. A few years ago I recalled how much fun it was and bought a used copy from Amazon since it is no longer marketed. It was an immediate hit with my grandchildren. Though they are both devotees of video games, they are perfectly happy in the analog world from time to time.

What our parents really preferred to play was card games. They were part of the Canasta craze in the early 1950s and occasionally went to a Canasta party in the neighborhood. Canasta could last for hours as the players worked towards 5000 points, and nothing today can compare with four adults sitting at a folding card table holding large hands of cards (as many as 15) as the smoke from their cigarettes filled the room. The haze soon began to resemble the drifting fog in a black and white horror movie. Later, the enthusiasts moved on to a more complicated version called Samba, which required more time to play and three decks of playing cards. Trying to shuffle 162 cards was not an easy task. Enterprising manufacturers soon introduced a variety of clever mechanical devices that shuffled the cards with just a few turns of a crank.

Our father eventually lost interest in Canasta, but our mother was almost always ready to sit down with her sons for a spirited contest (which she usually won). Dad much preferred to play a simpler game called Casino, and as soon as we had learned enough basic arithmetic to master the play, he taught us the rules. It's a game in which you take tricks by matching cards from your hand to those on the board, either by a direct match (eight takes eight) or combinations (an eight can take any cards whose combined total comes to eight). There are several ways to score points, but the general idea is to take the most cards. As in any card game, there is always the chance of the deal, but there is some skill involved. It's another game that has crossed generations. Both my children were enthusiastic Casino players and my granddaughter is now continuing the tradition.

In our grade school years, Saturday mornings frequently involved a trip to the YMCA near downtown. The Y offered a solid half day's entertainment in its ancient building dating from the early 1900s. The shower rooms had the lingering fragrance of old socks and Lysol with a hint of mildew. There were no lockers in the changing room. Instead, as you passed through the door, an attendant handed you a wire basket. You put your street clothes in the basket and took it back to the attendant, who handed you a brass tag on a string with the number that matched the one on the basket.

This meant our Catholic cohorts had two different trinkets hanging from their necks. For some reason, we were the only boys from Mary A. Todd who went to the Y. The boys we met there were largely from the East Side (which for all practical purposes was another planet as far as we were concerned) and were among the first Catholics we got to know since few went to Todd. Jon and I found the religious medals around their necks exotic. Such adornment was not part of the arrangements at Our Savior Lutheran. With a few encounters, though, we discovered Catholics were normal folk and whatever dire warnings we had heard about that faith were soon forgotten.

A Saturday morning at the Y was divided into three entertainments. First, we went to the gymnasium and played basketball, dodgeball or some other semi-organized game. Then we might run around on the elevated running track which circled the gym and was accessed by a perilous spiral staircase in one corner. There was also some ancient gymnastics equipment—a pommel horse and parallel bars—which was mostly too difficult and largely defeated us. I was much pleased when I was finally tall enough to climb on the horse. Other equipment which frustrated us included weights and climbing ropes. There was no instructor on hand—this was strictly a "free" period.

After an hour in the gym, now hot and sweaty, we went back to the changing room and got ready for a swim—also purely recreational. I am sure it would horrify many today, but the norm was to swim in the nude. We thought nothing of it—in fact, I did not own a swimsuit until I started going to camp several years later. The Y was very strict in insisting we use their towels. No doubt it was some sort of sanitary measure. Towel rental was five cents, and boys who didn't have the required nickel either went without or shared a towel with a friend. Whatever the diligence of the Y, it did not extend to the floors. My brother and I suffered from athletes' foot constantly during the school year when we were regulars at the Y. So much for careful hygiene.

After all this virtuous exercise we were ready for something more leisurely. For our final hour, we went to the game room. Choices involved ping-pong (one of our favorites), table hockey, skittles, and caroms for the active types. Those who were more cerebral inclined to checkers and chess. It was also time for refreshments and the standard snack was a bottle of Dr. Pepper (six cents—the machine had a nickel and a penny slot) and a bag of Planters Peanuts. The pop machine was on the cold side, and the soda invariably had slivers of ice, a feature which Jon and I found eminently satisfying. Before long the clock was inching towards noon, and we knew it was time to head home. We gathered our stuff, put on our coats and reluctantly passed through the doors to walk down the hill to the corner where our chariot, the Downer-Western bus, waited to take us home.

A few years later, the YMCA opened a brand-new building. It was clean, sparkling and much closer to our home. It had a much nicer pool, several gymnasiums, and many other improved features. But perhaps through that perverse streak which runs in humanity, neither of us ever took to that building and we never went to the Y again on a regular basis.

Learning the World

As a child, studying the atlas,
looking at the great world
spread across two pages,
I saw America in the center
and everything else to one side,
as was fitting and proper,
though parts of Asia and Russia
were repeated, both right and left,
which did not seem quite fair.
Top right were places I knew—
England, France, and Holland—
countries encountered in books,
understanding eased by similarities
(people who rode bicycles),
but below it was closer to enigma
as I read names which included
Morocco, Belgian Congo, and Malaysia—
but not entirely so, for I had stamps,
carefully mounted in my Scott's Album;
so I knew something of those environs:
knew of camels crossing the desert,
black men carrying boxes on their heads,
and rubber being collected from trees.
As I read further of these places
in my almanac and the Weekly Reader,
where cars and ice were scarce,
but apparently not the malevolence
of horrible disease and hidden beasts,
it was all a mix of fear and wonder,
of facts not easy to assimilate,
a grave threat to the quiet certainties
of a small boy in Aurora, Illinois,
attending second grade in 1952.

More Miscellanies

It would be hard to think of a store my brother and I appreciated more than the Fruit Juice House. In those days businesses were sometimes located in residential blocks (a practice that would trouble many people today). The FJH was across the street from our school and a few doors down from the Scafe's house, where I started my Cub scouting career. Our FJH was apparently one of several in Aurora at the time, though at the time I thought ours was unique.

I confess I can't recall a thing about fruit juice in this establishment. What I valued there was the ice cream (what seemed an infinite number of flavors) and the vast selection of penny candy. With just five cents, you could buy a bagful (in fact you got your candy in a small paper bag). As soon as school was over, anyone with money made a beeline to the FJH for some refueling. Among the big favorites were the sugar candies (especially the ones laid out in rows of dots attached to a wax paper roll), the paraffin wax bottles filled with colored sugar water, and flavored wax lips and mustaches. I am not certain any of that stuff could pass a *Consumer Reports* inspection today but it did not kill us.

The specialty merchandiser was very much the order of the day—unlike now when the Targets and Walmart's have largely driven them out of business. One of our favorites was Erlenborn's, an office supply place on River Street. We never tired of walking up and down the aisles, looking at the goods. Who could have guessed there were that many types of pencils, so many different colors of ink for fountain pens or so many ways to buy paper? There were staplers, scissors (large, small and left-handed), rulers of many different lengths, and we looked longingly at the boxes of colored pencils made in Germany, marveling at the luxury of having 36 different colors. I still have a box of Monarch staples with "Fits all standard size staplers and specially manufactured for Erlenborn's" boldly printed on the top of the cover. It has lasted me for a lifetime.

Another bunch of specialists could be found at the House of Vision, an optical store that made and fitted glasses. This outfit was especially important to me, as I was diagnosed with myopia by age four and in glasses for the start of second grade. During the growing years, my nearsightedness worsened rapidly, and I often had to have several changes a year. Throughout most of my years in Aurora (from age 6 until 21 or so), the same three people staffed the HOV, and to us, they represented the epitome of professional expertise. They fussed endlessly over the fit of the specs, repeatedly dipping the earpieces in a box of hot sand to make them pliable while the fit was being adjusted. When the optician was at last satisfied, you knew all would be well. Leaving the store in a new and stronger correction, there was always that momentary eureka experience as the world came into a new and sharper focus.

Undated picture of the author in front of 26 South Chestnut Street, probably summer of 1956. It appears that he may be shoeless, despite all the concerns over his footwear.

By the 1950s the independent grocers were on the defensive. The regional (Jewel T) and national chains (A&P) were the dominant players, but a few locals managed to hang on. There was one in our neighborhood—Maudsley's Clover Farm Store presided over by Dick Maudsley himself. Mr. Maudsley knew he could only survive by providing service the chains would not. He accepted phone orders, had a delivery service, was open on Sunday and provided charge account service. He also did a good business offering custom cuts of meat that might not be available at the larger stores. Our mother could place an order on the phone and dispatch us for pick-up without having to trust us with any cash.

Such was not the case with the bakery in the neighborhood—Ten Eyck—where I was sometimes sent to get various items. On these errands, I would carry a note with the order and whatever small sum was needed to cover the price. Over time Nelle got annoyed with the owners for unauthorized substitutions and suspected she was being overcharged when I was the receiving customer. Our business relationship with these folks eventually dried up, which was a shame, because the dinner rolls and the coffee cake were particularly tasty. One of the owners (a married couple from the Netherlands) might infrequently manage a smile and part with a sugar cookie, but in general, they acted as if courtesy was not an important element in customer service.

The Bourgos ate out often, and we had certain favorites depending upon the hour and the activity at hand. After a trip to Chicago, the Dutch Oven, a coffee shop style restaurant was conveniently located across the street from the train station. Entrees ranged from shrimp (1.50) or ocean perch (1.25) through the ham steak (1.50) or fried chicken (1.75), topping off with a T-bone steak for 3.25. The kids' menu came in at 75 cents for a hot dog and 80 for a burger. These prices included potato, vegetable (canned, of course) and a fresh roll with butter. Pie was the specialty of the house at 30 cents a slice and the beverage selection ranged from 10 to 20 cents. I know all these details because a Google search turned up a 1950s paper menu from this restaurant on sale for $22. In constant dollars, that was about $2.50 back then—enough to cover the ham steak, a cup of coffee, a slice of pie and a 15% tip.

The bill of fare at the Dutch Oven was typical of what was served at a local restaurant in smaller cities like Aurora in that day and age. Gourmet dining was mostly unknown. Unless you went to an Italian restaurant, the offerings were pretty much meat and potatoes. Restaurants often specialized around dessert offerings. Another place, the Fox Valley Restaurant, featured ice cream treats, culminating in the Belly Buster Sundae that cost a whole $1. My brother and I were always intrigued by this offering, but we never got a chance to try it.

On shopping days we might have lunch out, and our favorite, hands down, was the typical Greek restaurant (the variety without any Greek cuisine), the Best Ever Restaurant, where invariably we had the burger and fries. Another possible choice was Sylvester's Café, but it was second best as far as we were concerned because the place did not serve French fries. We also liked drugstore lunch counters, though their offerings were typically limited to a few sandwiches and soup from a can. They served our favorite phosphate—the infamous Green River—no doubt using food colors long since banned by the FDA.

If Aurora had any Chinese restaurants I was unaware of them, and pizza was something I did not become acquainted with until well into high school, as the only pizza place at that time was over on the east side of town, in a neighborhood where we rarely ventured. Most ethnic fare was unavailable unless you went into Chicago. There was the Bit O' Sweden, but aside from meatballs and the smorgasbord format, there was little about the fare that was Scandinavian.

But as far as eating out was concerned, my brother and I still mourn the passing of Prince Castle—a Chicago chain, which offered us the

Dutch Oven Coffee Shop

160 South Broadway

The menu from the Dutch Oven. As might be expected, the décor of the actual restaurant was not nearly as quaint and charming.

A la Carte

CHOICE T-BONE STEAK, Potato, Vegetable,
Homemade Roll and Butter 3.25

RIB EYE STEAK, Potato, Vegetable,
Homemade Rolls and Butter 2.45

GRILLED PORK CHOPS, Potato, Vegetable,
Homemade Roll and Butter 1.65

SMOKED HAM STEAK, Potato, Vegetable,
Homemade Roll and Butter 1.50

BEEFBURGER STEAK, Potato, Vegetable,
Homemade Roll and Butter 1.45

ONE HALF GOLDEN BROWNED
FRIED CHICKEN (disjointed)
Potato, Vegetable, Homemade Roll, Butter 1.75

ITALIAN SPAGHETTI PLATTER
A real treat, served with our special homemade
meat sauce covered with parmesan cheese, a
mixed green salad with french dressing — Homemade roll and butter 1.25

(A fresh mixed Salad with French Dressing
served with above Orders)

Sea Foods

FANTAIL FRENCH FRIED SHRIMP, From
the Blue Waters of the Gulf of Mexico, Fried to
a Golden Brown, Served with Cocktail Sauce,
French Fried Idaho Potatoes, Hearts of Lettuce,
Salad, French Dressing and Homemade Rolls and
Butter 1.50

FILLET of OCEAN PERCH, A Deep Sea Bone-
less Fish Delight Served with French Fried Idaho
Potatoes, Tartar Sauce, Tossed Green Salad,
French Dressing, Homemade Roll and Butter 1.25

Children's Specials

(under 10 yrs.)

"SMALL FRY"
Beefburger Patty,
Mashed Potatoes and
Gravy, Roll and
Kiddie glass of
Chocolate Milk

75c

"JIM DANDY"
Jumbo Frankfurter
Grilled French Fried
Potatoes, Vegetable
and Roll with Kiddie
Chocolate Milk

80c

(Minimum per Person — Charge 15c)

From Our Fountain

Delicious Ice Cream Milk Shakes .... .35

Rich Malted Milk Shakes .... .35

Ice Cream (dish) .... .20

Special of the month .... .25

Chocolate Sundae .... .35

Strawberry Sundae .... .35

Marshmallow Sundae .... .35

Ice Cold Coca Cola .... .15

Desserts

Large Delicious Fresh Baked Pies are available
on order . . .

Crust Pies 1.50

Cream Pies 1.65
(Deposit on pie tin) .50

We prepare and bake our Pies daily in our own
Sunlit Kitchens. We make our own pie fillings;
bake our own crusts — they are truly "homemade." Only the finest ingredients are used.

FRUIT, BERRY OR CREAM PIE .... .30

LAYER CAKE .... .30
(A la Mode .... 20c extra)

FRUITED JELLO .... .25

FRESH FRUIT IN SEASON .... .30 - .35
(Ask your waitress for the selection of the day)

Beverages

Fresh Hot Coffee (with Food Orders) .... .10

Hot Green or Orange Pekoe Tea .... .15

Iced Tea .... .15

Lemonade .... .20

Ice Cold Milk .... .15 - .20

Ice Cold Buttermilk .... .15 - .20

Hot Chocolate with Whipped Cream .... .20

Gourmet dining at its finest, and certainly none of the confusion that ensues
from an excess of choices.

"One-in-a-Million" malt. At Prince Castle, the ice cream was served in square blocks, using a unique dipping device. There were no tables—just a collection of chairs along the walls with a small tray attached to one of the armrests, much like the desks in college lecture halls. Aside from ice cream, the only thing they offered in those days were hamburgers, which cost 12 cents. Later they offered a larger burger for 24 cents, and still later, they started offering other varieties of sandwiches, fries, etc., in response to the arrival of McDonald's. It could not have been easy to do all that in the original building since it wasn't much larger than a couple of double garages shoved together.

There was no other competition in Aurora for the "slider" style burger until some outfit called Jet Burger opened a counter downtown not far from the Paramount Theater. It was popular for a while until it was discovered the burgers were being made from horsemeat. Thereafter, the Prince was once again supreme, but as far as we were concerned, there had never been any doubt.

Life Was Smaller Then

Here and there through these chapters, I have noted that many things today are much larger, more generously endowed or more expansive than their 1950s counterparts. In this interlude, I'll look at that issue more systematically.

First and foremost, we lived in smaller living spaces. In 2017 the average house is 2500 square feet and the average family consists of 2.6 people. In 1950, those figures were 983 square feet and 3.6 people. Today, college housing officials are bracing for a group of students who have never shared a bathroom—let alone a bedroom. In those days one bathroom was standard, and children were expected to share bedrooms with their siblings (as my brother and I did until I got to high school). There were still sizeable areas of rural America just getting dependable electrical service and indoor plumbing was still in the future for 25% of all American homes.

By necessity, then, rooms were much smaller. A double bed in many homes would eat up most of the space in even a larger bedroom. Unlike the gargantuan chairs and couches found in stores today, the furniture of that era had to be compact to fit in the available space. We lived for a while in a typical "home for heroes" (often called a cracker box house) built shortly after the war. It had four rooms and a tiny bath: a living room, a kitchen with a dining alcove, and two bedrooms. There was no central heating; instead, we had a wood burning stove in a little space off the kitchen, which was connected by vents to the other rooms, but it spread little warmth. Aside from bedtime, cold days in the winter were spent in the kitchen near the heat.

The concept of a separate entertainment or TV room was unknown; the ubiquitous "family" room was decades away. Along with the scarcity of bedrooms, privacy was often a luxury and TV a family matter since few households had more than one set. Hardly anyone had more than one phone either, which introduced all sorts of issues in terms of sharing (required) and again, privacy (seldom possible).

Smaller homes meant smaller and fewer appliances. We bought milk in quart bottles because the refrigerator could not accommodate larger sizes. Since the freezer compartment was minimal, our mother went to the store frequently since she couldn't afford to purchase more perishable meat and poultry items than could be used before they spoiled. Food was a lot more expensive in those days and claimed some 30% of the family budget. Today, that figure is less than 15% and a much larger share of it, perhaps 50%, goes to prepared food and restaurants. Prepared food in those days meant something in a can, Campbell's soup or cold cuts.

Food choices were much more limited at the grocery store. The average large grocery store had 2200 items on the shelves; today the figure is something like 17,000. Almost everything came in one variety and in much smaller packaging, both a function of cost and the size of our kitchens. Mayonnaise typically came in an 8 oz. jar, the only bottle of ketchup was 14 oz. and coffee was often purchased a half pound at a time.

Pepsi Cola ads in the 1950s made much of the fact that it was the first to introduce a 12-ounce bottle of soda. Coke waited sometime before they changed the traditional 6-ounce bottle. Jon and I thought 7-Up was neat because their bottle held 7 ounces. Fancy that—an extra ounce of fun—but our math was not so absurd. That extra ounce meant an increase of a whole 15%!

A lot of this rested on economic foundations that a trained specialist would explain better than I. The gist of it is that in the world of the 1950s, the cost of the materials in the jar of mayonnaise was a much higher percentage of the cost of the product than today. In our contemporary world, the lion's share of the cost (at least for ordinary consumer goods) is packaging, logistics, and marketing—which is why everything now comes in what would have been mega sizes in the world of my childhood. The cost difference of the ingredients and the production costs between X and 2X is negligible, and thus, the profit margin on 2X is greater.

The different economic circumstances of those days were also reflected in the elaborate packaging that was still available in the 1950s for a small additional cost. You could buy potato chips in large metal cans (handy for storing blocks, toy soldiers and other treasures), Nabisco saltines in metal boxes, and those wonderful Famous Chocolate Wafers in a metal tube. However, such frills were already receding, and the wise household manager (such as our mother) bought the fancy containers once and refilled them for years and years.

Another item that was costlier in those days was apparel, which claimed some 14% of the family budget. We did not have as many outfits then as people do today. This was especially true since attire was more formal in those days and there was a need for relatively expensive clothing such as suits for men and formal dresses for women. Clothing and shoes were repaired through the course of their lives and the dry cleaners and laundries got a lot of business because having a washer and drier in the house was less common, especially among apartment dwellers and those with smaller houses. In our early days in Aurora Mother sent our clothes out because there was no way to do the wash at home, and laundromats in Aurora were apparently still a few years off in the future.

When we consider that housing ate up 30% or so of the budget and add up the cost of other necessities, it is clear there was not much room for discretionary spending in those days, even for people like our parents who were well-settled in the middle class. Purchases were carefully evaluated, especially ones that involved significant money. There were no credit cards and borrowing money was generally avoided. While certain stores might offer installment payment plans, our family rarely used them. It was a cash-oriented world: many businesses refused to accept checks under any circumstances.

There were fewer temptations in those days. We had only broadcast TV or radio, which was free—in contrast with the charges for cable or satellite these days. Fast food was not generally available aside from a few burger joints. The concept of a $4 cup of "designer" coffee was inconceivable in a world where coffee came in one format (weak or strong depending on regional tastes) at 5 cents a cup. It was only several years after we moved to Aurora that Dad felt prosperous enough to start buying lunch instead of bringing a sandwich from home.

Travel was much slower, especially over long distances. The interstate system was not initiated until 1957 and many of the principal US highways still passed through the center of the towns on their routes. There were no jet airliners, which made flying overseas a trial for air travelers. Since the airliners of the day had limited ranges, a stop in Newfoundland or Iceland for refueling was needed. A flight to London or Paris could take 11 or more hours from the East Coast.

Most people today would also be amazed by the way we used the telephone. Local calls in town were unlimited and covered by the basic monthly fee, which also included the rental of the telephone itself. We could not own our own equipment (it wasn't permitted by the phone company) and one company (Bell Telephone) controlled some 80% of the phone service across the country. Innovation marched at whatever pace Bell thought suitable, and not according to any market pressures.

About 1958 or so we finally got direct dialing in Aurora. Before that, to make a long-distance call (which was pretty much any call outside of Aurora) you had to dial zero and talk to an operator. Even after long distance went self-service, the cost remained prohibitive for anything other than real emergencies. Telephone connections overseas, aside from a few large European cities, were often unavailable and what service existed was frightfully expensive. When our father went abroad, Mother fretted until she got the cablegram reporting he had safely arrived. This might take the better part of twenty-four hours after his plane took off.

Such delays and difficulties in communications led to several very trying experiences for our mother. The first was in 1954 and involved a simple misunderstanding over the day of departure. Dad left a day later than Nelle had assumed to be the plan. Thus, when his ostensible flight went down in the Atlantic and the accident was reported on the radio and in the papers, our poor mother was terribly alarmed. Fortunately, it was a weekday and Harza was open. She promptly called the office and the matter was immediately resolved. Jon and I were at home, but she somehow managed the poise to keep the matter to herself until the good news was confirmed.

The second incident took place in 1958 when our father and the rest of the Western community in Baghdad were forced to flee when a revolution broke out early one morning. Thanks to an alert American embassy, Dad was able to reach the airport before it closed and got away safely. Once again our mother heard the disquieting news hours before she knew he was safe. During the second crisis, Jon and I were at camp and blissfully ignorant of it all until we got a call from Aurora. A call from home? This was very much out of the ordinary.

A certain amount of morbid humor came to be associated with the long-distance call because it might mean the grave illness or death of someone near and dear. For non-essential or less critical messages, people still relied on telegrams or the postal service (a letter cost 3 cents and a postcard, two cents). Ironically enough, to send a telegram, you could telephone Western Union with your message, and when the reply arrived, they would call you and read the message over the phone. If you wanted a copy it was sent via mail and not the messenger boy of old movies.

Rumor even had it that Western Union no longer had all those dauntless telegraphers pounding out the Morse code. It was suggested the company used the phone to send your message to the destination city. But why not use the phone? AT&T, which owned the Bell System, owned Western Union as well. In those days Ma Bell still ruled the world.

The Medical Front

We grew in an era in which our health was a far less precarious matter than it had been for our parents. Inoculations for several diseases had been developed and penicillin and other antibiotics were available. We did not have to fear that a trivial infection would become fatally septic. Although preventives for childhood diseases such as mumps and measles were still some years away, serious illnesses like pertussis, diphtheria, and typhoid had been all but eliminated. The greatest fear of our early years was polio and a vaccine had been introduced by the mid-1950s.

By contrast, our mother had experienced firsthand the perils of childhood before the great advances in public health management and preventive medicine. She had several serious illnesses as a young girl, including typhoid fever. Each of her siblings had similar experiences as a young child. Her father's memoir mentions numerous occasions in which the elder Coggins were certain they were going to lose a child due to illness, and sadly enough, it happened at least three times.

We were largely spared from serious accident or illness (aside from the customary mumps, measles and so forth) in the early years, though my brother and I both had various encounters with maladies over the years. Jon had some early issues with asthma and over the years, more challenges while growing up than I. At age 12 he was diagnosed with an ulcer and ended up in the hospital. Unfortunately for him, the then current treatment ended up exacerbating his problems and he has had gastric issues off and on throughout his life. At age 14 or so he managed to break his wrist in a backyard football game and again landed at Copley Hospital.

There were several distinct differences from current medical practice. Today neither problem would necessarily dictate a hospital stay and with the ulcer, he was there for about a month. It was also tough because children were not allowed to visit, so on several occasions, he can remember going to the window to see me waving at him from down below.

I lost my tonsils at age three. In that age when medical generalists did a lot more than they do today, our family doctor did the operation at his office. Similarly, when I came down with appendicitis in the late summer of 1954, a general practitioner performed the surgery. Unlike today's overnight surgical recoveries, my hospital stay was lengthy (a week). I was anxious to go home, but my stay was certainly made easier by special attention and gifts from our mother, and by my roommate, an older boy (he was 13 or so) who seemed very grown up and who paid me the compliment of real conversation.

When I got home I was confined indoors for weeks, and that fall I was not allowed to resume physical education at school until November. I got weary of my sentence of imposed inactivity, but I do recall being anxious that my stitches would come out. Whether my fears were self-imposed or the result of dire warnings I cannot say, but they did not come to pass.

At some point, my brother developed an infection which was referred to by the sinister name of "blood poisoning." He had angry red streaks along his arm emanating from a cut or scrape that had gotten infected. There was every reason to be alarmed. Septicemia is no laughing matter and potentially fatal. Not so many years in the past, there would have been little that could be done in such cases. Jon's malady responded quickly to antibiotics and that was the end of the story.

There is nothing quite like a brush with death, real or imaginary, to bring a shiver of drama into the thoughts of a child. I certainly enjoyed entertaining my friends with accounts of my brother's narrow escape from the Grim Reaper—or of my own near-fatal encounter with the disastrous impact of a burst appendix.

Our first doctor in Aurora had his offices across the street and no doubt, convenience was the motive in going to him. He saw me through appendicitis and through an unfortunate encounter my skull had with a baseball bat (swung by one of my classmates during a moment of inattention). At some point, though, he got imperious with Mother over some medical problem my brother was experiencing. He went so far as to suggest the illness was all imaginary. She knew better, walked out of his office, and that was the end of our relationship.

On the recommendation of one of our neighbors, we switched to a doctor named Charles O'Connor. I recall him as a conscientious and capable GP and our parents remained under his care for the rest of their lives. There was always a certain fascination with Dr. O'Connor. Due to a childhood accident that allegedly involved some foolish behavior around a moving train, he had a prosthetic leg and a pronounced limp.

My memory, if accurate, is that a lot less attention was paid to preventive medicine in those days. We had to have up-to-date vaccinations at the start of certain school years and that might necessitate a trip to the doctor's office. I don't recall any experience like today's "well child" annual visit, just going when something was wrong. I am certain our parents did not bother with periodic checkup visits until later in life when both were suffering from chronic illnesses.

Our first dentist had his office in the second story of the same building occupied by our doctor. As with the doctor, I imagine proximity was our motive in choosing his services. He was a nice enough man, and I suppose he was a capable practitioner. What I remember most about him was that he discussed baseball with me and fancied himself an expert. However, I was equally serious and noted numerous factual errors in his pronouncements on the game and its heroes. I was shocked to discover that a man who claimed to be a diehard Cardinal fan did not know the year Stan Musial was born. It was 1920, for heavens sakes—not 1923 as he so confidently informed me. Of course, I said nothing in rebuttal, having been trained by our mother never to contradict an adult.

For reasons I cannot recall, we stayed with this practice for only a few years and then transferred our allegiances to a very nice man named Dr. Michaels. He then remained the family dentist for the rest of our parents' lives. I even came back to him as an adult a few times until I settled on a dentist in Chicago. On one of those last appointments (November 9, 1968), I was sitting in his chair when we experienced the tremors of an earthquake. To say that it was an unusual experience in Aurora is an understatement. One record I consulted noted only 11 significant earthquakes, all minor, in Illinois since 1838.

My memories of dentistry as a kid is sketchy, but I remember getting a tooth filled was a scary experience. In those days, the dentists were less generous with numbing agents. The first time I recall pain killer was when I had to have some teeth pulled as part of my orthodontic treatment. I also do not recollect that a lot of attention was paid to cleaning teeth as is now done on every routine visit. It was prior to the advent of the dental hygienist, and the dentist did just about everything himself, though he had an assistant who helped when he was doing a filling.

The experiences I had at the dentist's office paled by comparison with those at the orthodontist's. Orthodontics was a relatively primitive science in the 1950s and some of the techniques and technology were not easy to tolerate. The molds used to get a cast of the teeth employed a liquid plaster that set my gag reflex off. The brackets were a circular band installed on each tooth and sometimes coaxed on with a mallet. Frequent trips for tightening the wires and having to wear some sort of headgear at night were painful experiences.

The course of treatment was a long process. I was deemed a difficult case and I continued to visit the orthodontist throughout my high school years. In later years I had a retainer attached behind bottom incisors which did not come off until I was in my college years, which meant my orthodontic care must have stretched to ten years or so.

Over the years (no doubt thanks to parental instruction) I have generally been a compliant and cooperative soul. This was one of the few exceptions and perhaps the most blatant of my childhood. My only excuse is to think there must be at least one experience in everyone's childhood that was intolerable, and I chose to make this one mine.

The length of my sentence was no doubt affected by my resistance to the process. I was not dutiful about wearing the headgear and the rubber bands. From time to time, I would conspire to miss an appointment. I would have profited from following our mother's guidance—and no doubt, the orthodontist thought I was a highly uncooperative patient. That I was.

But there's a positive note to close on—Dr. John Ioratti—who was easily our favorite medical provider in those years. Dr. Ioratti qualified in the days when ophthalmology and ENT were still one combined specialty called "eye, ear, nose, and throat." So, he took care of both my terrible myopia and occasional complaints like earaches and sinus issues. All four of us had various vision issues, so we all visited Dr. "Johnny" at regular intervals. We were in complete agreement that he was one swell fellow.

Dr. Ioratti was a very thorough practitioner and a very kind and considerate man. Both Jon and I recall he always listened very carefully. Unlike some of our doctors, who would discuss our symptoms or complaints only with our mother (as if we were not in the room), he always wanted to hear directly from us. It could not have been easy to get a young child like me to tell him what I was seeing or not seeing in the eye exam, but he persevered, and I got the right correction.

A memory from my brother illustrates well what a special person Dr. Ioratti was. Years later, my brother was coming home from college with a terrible sinus infection. Mother called the doctor to see if Jon could drop by when he got home (of course was Ioratti's answer) but later learned his arrival was going to be delayed past the normal close of business. No matter, the doctor told our mother. He would stay until Jon could get there.

There is a certain amount of nostalgia about medical care in the past as compared with the present. People talk about house calls and other personal touches which seem absent these days, but even back then, a doctor who was willing to be inconvenienced like this for a patient was most unusual, indeed.

The Benefits of Autonomy

We profited enormously from our parents' belief that children should learn how to manage themselves as soon as possible. Over time we acquired a degree of freedom that might amaze parents of today, who have a much more cautious attitude about letting their children roam. From an early age, we were turned out to play in our own yard without supervision, our mother confidently assuming we would not be willing to risk her wrath by leaving the property. For the most part, she was correct.

Learning how to navigate the wider world began with the daily walk to school. By the time I was in second grade, I not only found the way to school on my own but had acquired the duty of dropping off my brother (age three) at his nursery school, which was in a church on the way to school. The church was only a block away, but he was a mischievous little fellow who could find all sorts of ways to bedevil his older brother. The latter was a rather grave soul, who did not always see the humor in such stunts, which included running away and at least once, lying down and refusing to move.

To get to Todd School we had to cross a major street, Galena Boulevard. Mother had a curious attitude about this street. In the early years, we were permitted to cross it at one intersection where there were stoplights if it were a trip to or from school. But for other activities, Galena Boulevard was an absolute frontier until I was in perhaps the fourth grade, at which point crossing was permitted, but *only* if we crossed at Locust Street where the traffic signal was. We discovered it was risky to violate these rules. On at least one occasion when we decided to cross elsewhere, one of her numerous informants turned us in, and the ensuing discussion was not pleasant.

As time went on, and we acquired bicycles, the world opened, and we were allowed to ride wherever we wished on the west side of town with just a few exceptions. Galena Boulevard was still off the charts, as were Lake Street (Illinois 31, another truck route) and the entire downtown. Once again, we discovered to our chagrin that

Nelle had spies on every corner. One day we decided it was silly to walk to the public library when we had perfectly good transportation. Trying to argue that the library was not technically downtown was to no avail.

A good deal of our freedom arose from our mother's attitude about what should occupy a boy's spare time. During the summer and on Saturdays during the school year, weather permitting, we were virtually expelled from the house as soon as breakfast was finished, with an admonition to return at noon. After lunch, it was the same process, with instructions about when to be home. If our father were in town, we were expected to be cleaned up and looking proper when he got home from the office. When he was overseas, the drill was more casual.

We often found ourselves outside, and it is in the nature of a boy to roam. As time went on and our universe expanded, we found many things to do. A few blocks away, there was an enormous freight rail yard, a major marshaling area for freight cars being transferred from the eastern rail lines to the western roads. Watching all the cars being moved around was always a good way to spend an hour. We might also decide to go downtown, to the library, over to the schoolyard to join a ball game, or just wander around looking for something of interest. I still recall how much fun it was to explore a street I did not know, such as my first visit to Palace Street, whose very name suggested mystery and power.

Over time our experiences went beyond our geographic freedom in Aurora. At ages ten and seven, we were dispatched to Boston for a spring vacation visit with Aunt Betty, Uncle Hugh and our two cousins, Tenna and Sandee. Mother took us to Union Station in Chicago and put us on the New York Central with several explicit instructions. First, we were to view the Pullman porter as our de facto parent (to make sure we had the proper attention she had reserved a roomette). Second, under no circumstances were we to leave the train until we reached our destination. Third, we were not to leave the station in Massachusetts with anyone except our aunt and uncle.

The trip was a great success. Our porter was a kindly fellow (I am sure he had been amply tipped in Chicago) who herded us off to the dining car at the appropriate times, reminded us to stay in our compartment at stops, and insisted we go to bed at a reasonable hour. It was a great thrill to write out the orders in the dining car, as one did in those days ("Strictly NO verbal orders," proclaimed the menu), to pay the bill ourselves and leave a tip for the waiter. As promised, Aunt Betty and Uncle Hugh were waiting for us when we pulled into Framingham. Going home, the process was reversed with Betty repeating Nelle's instructions to our porter. Since these two sisters were from a railroading family, they were at ease with the various customs and all went smoothly.

We had an enjoyable time in Boston. Our uncle took us to see the various shrines including the U.S.S. *Constitution*, the Old North Church, and Bunker Hill. We were amazed by the strange accents of all the people we heard, including our cousins and their father. The letter "r" utterly disappeared in their speech. We were also confused by some of the strange food choices in New England (clam rolls?) and a different vocabulary for certain items (what was a frappe, anyway?). Even familiar fare, like a hot dog, came in a different sort of presentation than in the Midwest.

Betty and Hugh, knowing our parents were religious about never fighting in front of us, staged a mock battle one day with her chasing him around with a frying pan, and managed to fool us completely. (At age 91, Hugh reminded me of this incident the last time I saw him.) Finally, Cousin Sandee inconveniently came down with some childhood disease (rheumatic fever?) local health laws deemed to require quarantine, and Aunt Betty always joked thereafter that she had to smuggle us out of town to get us home as scheduled.

At some point (perhaps I was 13) our mother decided we could take ourselves into Chicago for a White Sox game. I am sure she was relieved to forego the game, as she was never an ardent sports fan. I was excited about being entrusted with the leadership on this mission, but it also seemed a completely normal course of events. It certainly did not involve anything unusual or novel—I had already been to Comiskey Park numerous times.

The preparations for this trip were carefully rehearsed. We looked at the timetable and decided on the exact times for trains to and from Chicago. We talked about where and how to catch the #22 Clark-Wentworth bus that would take us directly to the park from Chicago's Union Station. We agreed on how much time would be necessary to get back to Union Station from the Southside in order not to miss the train home. Finally, all the expected costs were added up and I was entrusted with this sum plus a little extra, just in case of unexpected need. The voyage went off without a hitch (though the Sox lost, as they normally did in our company), and thereafter we took ourselves to the ballpark, though it was several more years before we could go into the city on our own without some specific plan for the venture.

Our parents were also devoted to the idea that summer camp was a highly useful experience in teaching us how to manage on our own. I first ventured away at age 11 to Boy Scout Camp, followed a year later by a trip to the Jamboree in Valley Forge. In 1958, at age ten, my brother was dispatched to the wilds of northern Wisconsin to Camp Ney-A-Ti. A few weeks later, after Scout camp, I joined him and thereafter, for several years, we both went off together for six weeks each summer. Many kids were escorted to camp by their parents, but not those intrepid Bourgo fellows. We were taken into Chicago to the Northwestern Station (which we thought a distinctly second-class operation compared to our Union Station) and handed over to the camp escort, who rode with us on the train to Summit, Wisconsin, some 250 miles north. Upon arriving at camp it was our duty to unpack our footlockers, unlike many bunkmates who had doting mothers on hand to look after this chore.

In truth, I think we felt sorry for those guys. This was a time when a guy did not need Mommy. Picking the right place to put the blue jeans and the T-shirts was something a man did for himself. This self-reliance, along with our geographic freedom, contributed to several major life skills. Both of us have always been handy at selecting the right equipment for any expedition, and we have both been adept in finding our route to the destination. From an early age, we knew that getting lost was not an acceptable option.

Mike and Jon on the front porch at 26 South Chestnut, summer 1957, just before Mike left for the Jamboree. I guess my brother didn't want me to leave.

The End of the Line

It was surely in June 1955
when my brother and I, adventurers,
wanted to see the end of the line.
Our mother, a believer in autonomy, agreed,
and not sure of the rules for round trips,
gave me twenty cents, four nickels,
twice the one-way fare. Just in case.
We walked to the corner, waited,
and boarded the Downer Place bus
at the near corner, on our side of the street—
unlike our downtown excursions—
and expectantly took our seats.
Soon, we were in unknown places,
beyond the three blocks we had explored,
passing houses we had never seen,
and though most were just houses,
there were chateaus of unexpected beauty
all across a wide expanse, ten minutes
filled with the marvels of gardens,
house numbers that passed 1500
and newly discovered lawns and trees.
Finally, we reached the last street,
the entire horizon in front of the bus
filled with an endless cornfield.
The bus stopped. The driver got out
and smoked a cigarette. He was in no hurry.
At last, he climbed back in, turned us homewards,
and through sights now familiar,
we soon spotted Healy Funeral Parlor,
pulled the cord, and emerged,
proven explorers safely returned,
having witnessed the known world—
and with ten cents to give back to our mother.

Campaigning for Stevenson (1952)

Adlai was our mother's distant third choice,
no equal to Kefauver and his coonskin cap,
and much less than President Harry,
but she was a loyal Democrat to her bones,
and dutifully volunteered for the crusade
to convince the American public
that Ike was no hero but a mere Republican.

Every Saturday afternoon that fall,
she marched us off to party headquarters,
an old storefront on a forgotten side street,
downstairs from the Odd Fellow's Hall,
an amalgam of old tables, six folding chairs,
buttons, folders, blue and white campaign posters
and old plank floors, worn smooth and gray.

No one came. The banks and stores closed at noon,
leaving downtown in the care of the bars.
As the afternoons crawled, I memorized
Democratic faces destined for November oblivion,
our mother gave up and read *McCall's,*
and I walked my brother from Lincoln to Broad,
counting parking meters and studying the sidewalk.

Each hour the local passed on the viaduct,
shaking the windows and rocking the floor,
the crickets sang in the doorway
and my brother napped in the empty display window.
From sunny days in late summer,
the dust dancing in the warm sunlight,
we passed into darkening October chill,
and no one came, not even an Odd Fellow.

Our Mother the Politician

Only over time have I come to realize our mother was a skilled politician. In my early years, I am not sure I understood what she was doing, though there was no doubt she was intensely interested in politics. I remember the 1952 national conventions (when I was seven) being reported on the radio. While she listened, she kept track of the votes with a scorecard she had cut out of the newspaper. That year she also had to endure the humiliation of wearing, albeit briefly, an "I Like Ike" button. It was presented to her with great fanfare by our father's employer, Mr. Harza, and she was diplomatically silent about her actual inclinations.

Thus, I grew up in a setting where politics and government were an important topic and frequently discussed. This set the stage for my lifelong interest in such matters. When 1966 rolled around and I was finally eligible to vote, having turned 21 the year before, my first ballot was a special occasion for Mother. By then I was living in Chicago and attending the University of Chicago but retained my permanent address in Aurora. I came out on the train on the morning of Election Day. At the polls, she beamed as she told all and sundry that I was casting my initial vote. We then went out to lunch and celebrated with a cocktail before I went back to Chicago. Shortly thereafter, I changed my registration and cast the first of two votes for Richard J. Daley—no surprise since a fundamental part of my political upbringing involved an unwavering allegiance to the Democratic Party.

In Tennessee, where she lived until we moved north in 1951, she had not voted. The reason was a Southern practice called the poll tax. Although the nominal amount per year was modest, it was cumulative if not paid. Like many people, she skipped paying during the Depression and before long, her obligation was a meaningful amount in an era when 75 cents an hour was a decent wage. In addition, she once told me, Southern women rarely participated in the political process. It was considered "unladylike."

Accordingly, our relocation freed her to pursue some very definite interests. In 1952 her friend and neighbor, Sally Doane, recruited her to work for the Stevenson campaign. She quickly discovered that being a Democrat in solidly Republican Kane County, Illinois, condemned one to an almost endless prospect of second place finishes. This was reinforced during one election cycle when she and Sally had to drive all over town, visiting multiple polling places to sign off on the totals, since there were simply not enough Democratic activists for every precinct, and the law required both parties supply witnesses to certify the results.

Consequently, she shifted her interests to school matters. As a relief worker in Kentucky during the Depression, Nelle had personally witnessed the desperation and grinding poverty of people with little schooling. Further, she had lived for a long time in a state with a lukewarm commitment to public education, which she found appalling and inexplicable. Initially, her involvement was as a PTA officer. Her discovery that the District 129 school board was saddled with a majority of old fogies whose agenda was low taxes rather than quality schools was motive enough for her to enter the arena of school elections.

By 1954 or so, she was already involved in her first election. Working with several other PTA colleagues, she recruited candidates (including our veterinarian) who she thought would do an admirable job as board members. Next was the job of organizing a successful election campaign. Then as now, school elections got little attention and often attracted only a small percentage of the eligible voters. There was always a vocal minority of people who felt they were already paying too much in taxes and whose contention was that most of their tax dollars were being wasted since (as everyone knew) government was incompetent by definition. And naturally enough, the naysayers could always be counted to show up at the polls, and low turn-outs certainly played to their advantage.

It took Nelle no time to figure out that the key to success was getting more voters to the polls. Over time she built up a formidable political machine that got her voters to the polls and almost always succeeded in getting her candidates elected. There were three major elements in her organization: a schedule of "meet the candidate" events held in people's homes, elaborate calling trees to remind people about the election and urge them to vote, and a team of drivers on election days to ferry the voters to and from the polls.

There was nothing unique about this strategy. It was Politics 101 but required a good deal of organizational effort and the recruiting of volunteers to host the meetings, make the calls and drive the cars. Recruiting was one of Nelle's real skills. She would spend hours on the phone talking to people and persuading them to work with her. I can still recall a conversation I overheard one day when she was trying to convince some reluctant person that hosting a coffee klatch for a candidate was not an impossibly difficult chore. After countering numerous objections, I could tell she was getting impatient. Finally, she offered to come to the first meeting and demonstrate the art of holding an event that would allow the candidate to present himself in the best possible light. That did the trick, and I don't believe she had to make good on her offer.

She was less successful with referendums and votes on bond issues. Since these involved an explicit message of higher taxes to pay for the proposed improvement, the "no" element was much more committed to defeating the proposals. Through her PTA connections, she was quite aware of the resources the better school districts had and she developed an agenda she promoted for many years. Though success eluded her at times, by the time of her death in 1983 she had the pleasure of seeing almost every aim realized, including a new middle school, an auditorium and swimming pool at the high school, more teachers and smaller class sizes, and expanded curricula. It was a record of which she could be justly proud.

The other side of her political career was serving as a PTA officer. In school board matters, Mother was more than content to remain a back-room player. Despite urgings from her friends, she did not want to be elected to the board. The PTA was a different matter. She was over time elected President of a PTA unit seven times, serving as chief executive in every school I attended, and later rising to district President. She served on the Illinois state board of directors for a number of years, and a highlight of every spring was the state convention, which she enjoyed greatly. Only in later years when I had become an adult and she would talk about that year's convention program, her old friends around the state and the various educational issues on her mind, did I finally grasp how involved and well-connected she was with education policy in the state.

Politics and PTA were not her only community service activity. Over the years she was deeply involved with the hospital, the YWCA and the Red Cross. She spent many hours in these efforts and held positions of responsibility in all three organizations at various times. How she found time to do all this is a marvel. I can only imagine how full her calendar must have been over the years. Yet, neither my brother nor I ever felt we were being neglected, and she was always attentive to our progress in school and the like.

As a successful political boss, Nelle was keenly aware of the need to recognize and reward her team. There wasn't anything tangible she could offer anyone. Unlike Mayor Daley, she did not have a treasure trove of jobs or contracts to hand out, but she knew everyone loved a party. Thus, one of the annual rituals in our home for several years was the Christmas soiree for all her various friends and allies, which included her campaign crew, board members and various teachers and administrators. I can still recall how packed the house seemed those nights and how the party got noisier as the evening went on, and bowl after bowl of eggnog punch disappeared.

Though we were officially exiled to the second floor, we managed to get in more than a few peeks and were quite titillated by the sight of those pillars of rectitude having a drink, smoking cigarettes, and—what a sight—laughing. Who knew Mr. A or Miss B ever laughed? Such levity was scarce when we saw them at school. However, we knew the code of silence and we adhered to it. We never had the fun of telling someone at school that we had seen teachers acting like normal humans.

Ready for Christmas, 1956

The Activist (1905-1983)

Moving to the north with her family in '51,
liberated from the poll tax and gentility,
her thoughts moved in civic directions.
After Depression days in Harlan County,
a relief worker among desperate miners,
she found no charm in the flowers of ignorance,
and the schools became her public place.

Nelle apprenticed with the local PTA
(over the years elected a president seven times),
and found the villains soon enough—
the mossbacks on the school board
who valued taxes more than teaching.
Content to remain a backroom player,
she recruited candidates and went to work.

Managing her moves from the hall phone,
fueled by endless cigarettes and stale coffee,
she found the parts and built her machine,
a great web of telephone calling trees,
coffee klatches and election day drivers.
Year after year her candidates sat on the board
while her opponents got to watch.

 After twenty years, she retired and looked back
at new buildings, a pool, an auditorium,
more teachers, modern curricula and, she hoped,
a few minds changed in Springfield.
The fall before her death she returned,
a once weekly classroom volunteer,
immediately a high point in her week:
she had, of course, been called home.

Chicago: The Later Years

About the time I turned 12 or so, the annual Christmas break in Chicago became a tradition. A day or two after Christmas, we would go into the city, check into a hotel (at first the LaSalle and later the Bismarck), and stay until New Year's Day. True enough, we only lived 40 miles from the city, but Dad enjoyed a break from the daily two-hour commute, and our mother got time off from the kitchen plus plenty of leisure for shopping. We got to experience more and more of the city as our parents increasingly turned us loose to find our own entertainment as we got older.

I am sure this would be strange to some parents—the notion of letting two boys of our age (I would have been in 7th or 8th grade) wander around downtown Chicago—but mine never had the least concern about our safety or our ability to stay out of trouble. There were no long sermons about the sins of the city and just a cursory discussion of the rules. Somehow, they were confident we would not venture too far south into Skid Row or try to sneak into one of the adult movies in the south end of the Loop.

In this assumption they were correct. I was a curious child but not an especially brave one—walking by one of those theaters and peeking at the notices was about as far as I would go. In any event, we would have never been able to get in. As I later learned, such places were very careful not to admit minors and their reason for prudence had everything to do with staying in business. By the letter of the law in the 1950s, what they were showing was illegal. Part of their peace treaty with the cops was an explicit understanding that minors would not be admitted.

My brother and I loved to go to the movies in Chicago. There were still several enormous palaces in the Loop (The Chicago, The Oriental, and The Roosevelt) and we marveled that the movies started at 9 AM. In the early days, they still had ushers to show you the way to a seat, awfully handy in the balcony at the Chicago, where the steps were so steep that one worried about falling off into the orchestra seats below. During our Christmas stay, we usually managed to get in at least two movies. I recall "The Seventh Voyage of Sinbad," starring the immortal Kerwin Mathews and Kathryn Grant, "The Buccaneer" with Yul Brynner and Charles Boyer and "Tom Thumb" with Russ Tamblyn among the many we saw. After the early movie, we would often meet our parents at some restaurant or a Fields dining room for lunch.

The other aspect of movies in Chicago was the limited showing. In those days, a fair number of movies had long runs (sometimes a year) at specialty theaters before their general release, especially features that used some special film technology like Cinerama (an early and a rather crude version of IMAX). There were two smaller theaters up on the near north side that ran these movies. Over the years we saw such films as *Oklahoma, The Greatest Show on Earth, Around the World in Eighty Days* and *Lawrence of Arabia* in one of these limited run houses. My brother and I were happy to see such movies, usually with the parents, but we were not pleased with the refreshment arrangements. Theaters like these did not sell popcorn and soda. Still, if the parents were feeling generous you went home with a special souvenir book that gave you all the details on how the film was made and assured you the movie you had just seen was about the greatest ever produced in Hollywood.

After lunch with Mom and Dad, if we did not go to another movie, the penny arcade in the Greyhound terminal at Randolph and State was at the head of our list. As far as we were concerned it was top notch entertainment to move from game to game, shooting pinballs, firing guns, driving auto simulators and all the rest. The population was a curious mix of children and adults, many of them either soldiers or sailors who were in transit, or just downtown for some recreation while on leave. There were both an enormous Navy training station (Great Lakes) and an Army base (Fort Sheridan) near Chicago and the Loop was always awash in young men in uniform. This was the era of draftees, and my brother and I were nonplussed on several occasions when we talked to a would-be hero who gave us a thoroughly disgruntled perspective on serving one's country. Although we had heard Captain Al Bourgo speak irreverently about his Army days, we nevertheless assumed being a soldier was always an exciting and worthwhile experience.

In time, Jon and I might be completely on our own for the day, and free to pick our own lunch spot. We soon discovered we had a clear favorite: Tad's Steakhouse. Tad's was a chain operation that apparently still has outlets in New York and San Francisco, but no longer in Chicago from what I can determine. The menu at Tad's was simple. It was a steak, a baked potato, a salad and a piece of garlic bread. Food was served cafeteria style and the diners carried their food to the table on a tray. The only decision necessary was rare, medium or well done, and the price was modest ($1.99 or so the first time we went) —as no doubt, was the quality of the steak— but we thought the food was wonderful.

At Brookfield Zoo. The polar bears were a big favorite as (incredibly enough) the public was permitted to toss them treats. They were partial to caramel corn.

There were always plenty of things to do besides the movies and the arcade. As we left the arcade, the next store to the west was some sort of bargain variety store with window displays of knives and other interesting discount paraphernalia we thought worth a detailed

137

perusal. It was one of those places with a semi-permanent sign that screamed, "Losing Our Lease! Everything Must Go!" Kroch and Brentano's was a fantastic book store and always a good place to pass time browsing through all the aisles. I was amazed to discover the store sold books in languages other than English. Who were the people who knew how to read those secret codes?

We also loved to peruse the aisles in stamp and coin stores (John G. Ross was our favorite) or in the stamp department at Field's, salivating over all the rare and beautiful issues. It astounded us there were people who would pay $25 for a single stamp. I was certain I'd never have that kind of money. Another special place was Abercrombie and Fitch, a store entirely unlike the chain that carries its name today. A & F was a high-end sporting goods, camping gear, and outdoor clothing place. My brother and I were fascinated by the elaborate cases for fishing tackle and the incredibly arranged picnic baskets with all the necessaries for serving anything from beer and hot dogs to caviar and champagne. It was another place that never disappointed, and I always wondered who the people were that bought its merchandise.

Walking through the Loop was like walking between walls; the tall buildings that lined virtually every block turned the streets into caverns. Downtown Chicago was always shady from morning to night. The sun could not find its way into the north-south streets, especially in the winter. It would have been light if we had wandered east to Michigan Avenue, the last street before Grant Park and the Lake, but we rarely left the Loop. Today, the downtown retail center of Chicago has migrated east and north along Michigan, but in our day there was little there aside from hotels, Symphony Hall, and exclusive men's clubs—nothing that appealed to us.

Another favorite trip to the city involved going in for the Sunday brunch at the College Inn in the Sherman Hotel. The College Inn was one of Chicago's oldest night clubs, but on Sunday mornings the place was oriented to the younger customer. A waiter dressed up as a cowboy named Skipalong and a genuine Native American in full regalia wandered through the restaurant talking with the customers and entertaining the kids with jokes, patter, and so forth. At one point we had a photo of ourselves posed with the cowboy and Indian, but like many treasures, it has not survived. There were two things on the menu we loved—the Shirley Temple cocktails and the toasted cocktail rye. The latter had a flavor that I have not forgotten more than sixty years later.

One of our strangest Chicago adventures involved a visit to the Pacific Garden Mission, a storefront homeless shelter/church operation located in Skid Row on South State Street. I was not terribly pious as a boy, but I was a sucker for rescue and redemption. Any rags to riches or sin to salvation story could hold my attention. And why not? My native land has always had much more faith in the ability of people to direct their lives than jaded and cynical Europe. In America, falling victim to fate means you weren't trying hard enough—or you needed a little more training.

The mission sponsored a weekly radio drama entitled "Unshackled." Each week the plot was about the same—the story of someone who was able to change directions with the help of a new-found faith in God. The only thing that differed was the difficulty they were in before the transformation: drugs, alcohol, poverty, crime and other assorted ills came and went over the weeks. Just when the hero or heroine of our story had reached the nadir of their existence, they would suddenly see the light, start to believe and presto! Before long they were back on their feet and prospering. Each story featured a wise mentor, in the form of a friend, a relative or a minister, whose advice was spurned several times before the denouement.

This program was regular fare in our house, and I grew curious about an institution that appeared to have so much power to help people out of their dilemmas. In addition to the dramatized story, each program had commercial breaks in which we heard real-life stories of the people who were rescued from disaster by the kindly and knowing souls who directed the Pacific Garden Mission—plus polite requests for donations.

I became obsessed with the idea of seeing the mission. It was, as I pointed out to our mother, just a few blocks from places we frequented in Chicago. Finally, she relented and a visit to the holy shrine was promised on our next trip into Chicago.

As we set off down State Street, I noticed how much the setting changed as soon as we got south of Van Buren (and officially out of the Loop). The buildings became shabby, and the people even more so. They were almost all men, standing around doing nothing or sitting in door fronts. Not one of them looked happy or was smiling, I was sure they were all staring at us—a respectably dressed woman with two grade school boys—and I can still recall asking myself if this had been such a hot idea. I am sure I was hanging on tightly to that capable maternal hand. It felt like miles (it was actually a few short blocks south of the Loop) but eventually we reached the front door and went inside.

Our host could not have been kinder. He was a staff member of some sort and was quite pleased when Nelle explained the reason for our visit. We then received a lengthy and detailed personal tour of the facility, showing us the dorms, the dining room, the study rooms, and the chapel. I was awestruck with the effort and infrastructure needed to rescue a soul. No one was as admirable to me as a person like our guide, who was in my eyes a genuine expert.

Our tour over, we went out the door and turned north on State. Some well-dressed fellow stopped us and asked our mother if she knew where she was and whether she was lost. Very politely but firmly, she advised him the answer was yes—and no—she knew perfectly well what she was up to. It came as absolutely no surprise to me. I never doubted even for an instant she knew what she was doing, either then or now. Whether in Buenos Aires or Bucharest, Nelle C. Bourgo would have gone about her business with an air of confidence and would have never doubted her ability to reach her destination.

Before Television

Life was no less happy or tragic,
and then as now, days had 24 hours,
but the news was delivered on paper,
entertainment arrived on the radio at home
or the movie screen downtown,
and we learned what people looked like
in the pages of *Life* Magazine.

The day began with the Chicago *Tribune*,
a great sports page and wonderful comics,
and then Don McNeill and the Breakfast Club.
After the school day, we rushed home
for the Lone Ranger and Tonto at 4:30,
and the day ended with the *Beacon News*,
which had lousy sports and awful comics.

On Saturdays, our mother could negotiate
an afternoon of peace with a dollar in change,
which generated bus fare, popcorn, candy,
the latest Randolph Scott western,
Bugs Bunny, and a newsreel where we saw
movie stars playing on the beach,
the Queen in her palace and Ike on the course.

In time, the old order began to fall apart
as the Cisco Kid and Sergeant Preston vanished,
and Wednesdays we'd pray for an invitation
from one of the neighbors to watch Disney.
After years of resistance, the old man gave in,
bought a 21" Philco in Colonial Maple,
and we were now citizens in the new age
of Howdy Doody and Marshall McLuhan.

Entertainment

I grew up at a time when television was just emerging, but thanks to our parents' opposition to acquiring an "idiot-box" (as Dad termed it), we had to make do with other means of entertainment until our first television appeared. It was no coincidence the TV arrived just in time for the Bears/Giants NFL title game in December 1956 and the 1957 New Year's Day bowl games. Our father always enjoyed football, and our mother was especially pleased to get to watch the Rose Parade. My brother and I were not keen on the parade, but we watched some of the football.

When the TV was finally in place, it was an immediate hit with all concerned. Mother immediately found favorites among the daytime quiz shows, Dad leaned to Ed Sullivan and "What's My Line," and my brother and I predictably favored westerns, cartoons, and sports. We also enjoyed re-runs of the classic "Flash Gordon" serial starring Buster Crabbe and we were both great fans of Rocky and Bullwinkle. About this time we also became entranced with the idea of trying to stay up all night. Trying to use the TV as a stimulus to fight off the drowsies was only partially successful since in those days most stations went off the air about midnight.

The entire family enjoyed the evening quiz shows and we all followed some of the famous battles on the "$64,000 Question" and "Twenty-One." Mother and I were both crushed when it was revealed our hero, Charles Van Doren, had won by cheating. No doubt she was able to ease some of her disappointment by watching her favorite bowlers. Even as a child I was amazed by her sudden interest in this sport, since one, she had never previously shown the slightest interest in any sport and two, I am certain she never spent a moment in a bowling alley.

Until I was 12 (and Jon 9) it was incumbent upon us to find other means of entertainment. We were highly aware of TV from after-school visits with friends who had a set (every family except ours seemed to have one) and from invitations from a neighbor to come watch a show. In the latter category, my brother and I always hoped the lady who owned the boarding house up the alley would invite us over to see the Disney show, which began at 6:30 on Wednesday evening. This only took place when our father was out of town. When he was in residence dinner was on the late side, about 7:00, which meant no Disney. Since he was usually away more weeks of the year than home, we got to watch Tinker Bell waving her magic wand on many occasions.

I found after school TV disappointing. I thought "Howdy Doody" and "The Mickey Mouse Club" were dopey. Sky King was not too bad, but Roy Rogers was my least favorite cowboy and Gene Autry wasn't much better. I knew you couldn't shoot a gun out of a bad guy's hand as often as they did it. On *The Roy Rogers Show*, there was a dumb jeep, a dumber guy who drove it, and Dale Evans, whose main job was to sing drippy songs. TV could not compete with the movies when it came to the business of real Western heroes.

Not having a TV could be a source of discomfort. Aside from my envy of people who had one, it led to discomfort at school when the other kids talked about what Lucy had done the night before, or even more embarrassingly, when a teacher asked me what I thought of the Milton Berle show and I had to admit the awful truth. Perhaps the pinnacle of this discomfort was in early 1953, on the occasion of Eisenhower's inauguration. Sensing an evil era coming to an end, the powers-that-be in Republican Aurora decided school would be excused on Inauguration Day so that all students could watch the ceremonies and write reports in class the following day. Since I was one of the few kids in my class without a TV, I became a charity case who had to be passed off to a classmate whose family allowed me to come to their house to witness the festivities.

For some years the radio was our substitute for television. In the early 50s, the networks had not yet surrendered radio to the disk jockeys or the talk shows. Drama, news and even a few variety shows were still available. On Saturday nights the Lux Radio Theater still offered abridged movie plots with the actual stars playing their parts. Late in the afternoon after school, we could hear the Lone Ranger, Sergeant Preston, and the Cisco Kid. After dinner, the radio was usually off limits, but we might occasionally manage to sneak in "Gunsmoke" or some cops and robbers, though our mother was not too keen on either, as she thought their realism and violence too much for our tender ears.

Unlike his reluctance to accept television, our father was an early stereo enthusiast and welcomed the advent of long-playing records. He loved good music and his tastes were wide-ranging from opera, Broadway musicals, organ classics by E. Power Biggs (I am told that when I was three or so, I would ask him if we could listen to Biggy Powers), and Gypsy violin music to Frank Sinatra. I can still see him sitting in his easy chair on a Sunday afternoon marking time with his hand while listening to an aria from *I Pagliacci* or the songs from *Kismet*. He liked music during dinner, especially big band dance music or one of Jackie Gleason's many mood music albums.

He had a special love for French popular music, and his collection included Michel Le Grand, Jacqueline Francois and cabaret singers like Patachou. During one of his many sojourns in Beirut, when the city was still the "Paris of the Levant," he had the great thrill of meeting Jacqueline in person at the club where she was appearing, a story he never tired of remembering.

Unlike my peers, who started listening to WLS, the first top 40 station in Chicago, I was uninterested in the pop music of the day. I was much older and in my college years before I started to appreciate rock music. Since that time, I have become an Elvis fan and made the pilgrimage to Graceland, even though the King failed to impress me in his early years. Jon and I did go to Elvis's first movie, fittingly enough a Western, and we both liked it. It did have Richard Egan, who was one of our favorite action film stars.

More than anything else, though, it was the movies we really enjoyed. Our childhood was at the tail end of the golden age of movies, that era before TV began to take off and cut into the monopoly Hollywood had over filmed entertainment. There were no multiplex theaters; the theaters were still downtown and played one movie at a time, which usually changed every Friday. In Aurora, we had two first-run theaters (the Paramount and the Isle) and a third, the Tivoli, which showed "B" movies and second runs. No presentation was complete without previews, a newsreel, and a cartoon. If the feature movie was on the brief side, there might be a short subject, usually a farce such as the Three Stooges.

Going to the movies (or as Nelle said, "the picture show") then was a more casual activity than today. Once you bought your ticket, you could stay as long as you wanted. There was no intermission between showings and no effort made to clear out the audience after each showing. We also thought nothing of going to a movie already in progress and remaining until we reached the point where we had come in. If it was a movie we really liked, we might stay and watch until we reached the end again.

We went to the movies on a regular basis during my grade school years, perhaps twice a month or more, depending on what was playing. At first, we only went if our mother wanted to take in a show. Though her favorites were musicals and comedies, she also enjoyed bio-pics, especially if the subject was a celebrity. Consequently, we saw a whole string of such films about Benny Goodman, Eddie Cantor, and so forth. In keeping with her love of musicals, she was crazy about Judy Garland and a fan of such performers as Donald O'Connor, Dan Dailey, Gene Kelly, Gordon McRae, and Shirley Jones.

She also enjoyed tearjerkers like "A Star is Born" or "The Last Time I saw Paris." As a small boy, I was very concerned with her tears at the end of the latter film. I can recall being more than a little alarmed—after all, parents are not supposed to cry. (A few years ago I watched it again and I confess my eyes got moist, too.) I think she was generally more pleased with films like "Picnic" that had a happy ending. Another favorite was a series comedy like "Ma and Pa Kettle" or "Francis the Talking Mule." There were seven editions of Francis and ten of Ma and Pa, and I suspect that we managed to take in just about all of them. She did not much care for heavy drama (such as adaptations of Tennessee Williams), mysteries or thrillers. She was not keen on Alfred Hitchcock; I think she may have found him suspect in the morals department, as she was quite straight-laced—and not at all pleased in her later years as movies started to cross into territory the Hayes Code had blocked off for many years.

By the time I was ten or so, my brother and I started going to the movies on our own. Mother gave us a dollar and sent us on our way, with a definite plan as to which movie we were going to see. Certain genres were out of bounds: horror shows, murder mysteries, and prison films were among the verboten categories. None of this bothered us much, as our favorites were Westerns, adventure stories like "Journey to the Center of the Earth," baseball movies, and medieval romances like "Ivanhoe" or "Knights of the Round Table." We were also keen on war movies, especially those involving the Air Force, such as "Battle Hymn" and the "Bridges of Toko-ri."

"Ok, you varmints—you're dealin' with the Bourgo Boys." Appears that we have passed on the six shooters in favor of carbines.

Another aspect of the movies was the Saturday morning marathon cartoon show. Starting in the morning the program included a large number of cartoons plus several short subjects or serials such as the Bowery Boys, Flash Gordon or the Three Stooges. Our preference was the Bowery Boys and no matter your favorite cartoon characters—Tom and Jerry, Bugs Bunny and Daffy, Heckle and Jeckle or good old Foghorn Leghorn—you were sure to get at least one chance to enjoy them. Some of those cartoons would be strange to the kids of today, such as Mighty Mouse or Casper the Friendly Ghost, but we thought they were fine. During the intermission, a guy would come out on the stage and demonstrate tricks using yoyos, paddle balls, and other such items. After the show, these gadgets were on sale in the lobby.

The impact movies had on our imaginations was considerable. For days after a good film, our play would be centered around re-enacting all the thrills we had seen on the screen. Like any kids of that era, we were well equipped with the gear for Western adventure. Medieval movies forced us to improvisation—such as using broom handles for lances and garbage can lids as shields. The occasional space opera (such as Flash Gordon) inspired us to become inventive with cardboard, tape and other materials to fashion a rocket ship.

There was no doubt in our minds that a good Western was the epitome of cinematic art. By far and away our favorite cowboy actor was Randolph Scott. In the 1950s Scott made at least one new film every year and we were always there to watch him defeat the bad guys. Unlike scrubbed up heroes such as Roy and Gene, Scott's characters were more complex and unpredictable. They were often not cheerful fellows and not above a bit of guile to win the day. They were often loners who had issues with the law-abiding as well as the lawbreakers. Scott was already in his fifties and little attempt was made to conceal it. One look at that wrinkled, leathery face and you knew this was a guy who had been through a lot.

Our dollar was carefully spent. Admission was twenty-five cents for kids, so that amounted to half our money. Popcorn was 15 cents apiece, which took the total spending up to eighty cents. That left twenty cents or enough for a round trip on the bus downtown. If the weather was nice, though, my brother and I might decide to walk home and spend the remaining ten cents on candy bars. A few years after we moved to Aurora, there was a vast improvement in the business of popcorn. The theaters had not yet instituted their ban on bringing in food from outside, and a fine enterprise by the name of Kaskey's Korn Krib opened near the Paramount Theater. Not only did they sell a superior product, but the price—10 cents—meant we no longer had to give up our lift home if we wanted a Snickers bar. If it were a nice day, we might forego that bus ride and enjoy the guilty pleasures of a second candy bar. Besides, the walk home had its own rewards. You never knew what you might chance to see.

Toys

Then as now, toys were an important part of growing up. However, they were a good deal more expensive than they are today and we probably had fewer possessions than the typical child today. They were also a lot sturdier, and not nearly as safe. This was a time when children traveled in cars without any safety restraints and the same laissez-faire spirit prevailed in the toy business.

Our parents were generous and we never lacked for entertainment or diversion in the matter of toys. Christmas morning seemed like an endless cornucopia of new treasures, and unlike the Grinches of legend, they did not use the holiday (or our birthdays) to disguise pajamas as a gift. The only apparel that arrived in this manner was something special like a cowboy shirt or a baseball jacket that was on the want list. Otherwise, clothing was considered a commodity and acquired as needed.

I simply can't recall all the various things I had but there were some real favorites I have never forgotten. There were also some toys we never got around to using as intended. We had an Erector Set but I don't remember anything of note ever getting constructed unless our father got involved. Perhaps like fathers in all ages, he had picked it out because he thought he would like to play with it. Other construction sets like Tinkertoys and Lincoln Logs were more suited to our skills and got a lot of use.

I suspect Dad might have been entertaining similar thoughts when he picked out our electric train. He opted for an HO gauge from a German company called Marklin. Most people bought the larger American scale trains made by Lionel and American Flyer, but as he told us, we could get an awful lot more rails into any given space with the smaller HO sized train. Jon and I were both very fond of playing with the train and eventually we had a large piece of plywood on sawhorses where the track layout could be left assembled. Until this time, though, we always laid out an oval of track near the Christmas tree each year in anticipation of new cars (or perhaps a new engine!) making an appearance on Christmas morning.

Having a European electric train was a mixed blessing. The train itself was easy to use, durable (it was still running fifty years later when I finally sold it) and pleasantly exotic with its signage in foreign languages, but sometimes I did think it would be nice to have cars with some of those logos we loved to spot in American railroad freight yards.

Sports games were favorites as we got older. None of the commercial baseball replicas ever attracted our fancy quite like an informal low-tech baseball game we picked up at Camp Ney-a-Ti. It was played with a baseball diamond ruled out on a piece of plywood, four dice, and buttons for base runners. A detailed chart provided the results for each at-bat after you had thrown the four dice (four of a kind or 23 was a homer). Like the real thing, our contests were nine innings long with three outs per side. We played every day at camp during the after-lunch rest period, keeping detailed stats on our lineups and playing for a cabin "pennant."

For basketball, we had a game constructed of cardboard that used springs to propel a ping pong ball towards a basket mounted at each end of the court. There was a bit of art in scoring a basket. Too much pull on the lever that launched the ball, and you sent it flying across the room. Too little, and the resulting airball turned things over to your opponent as the board was tipped to let the ball roll into one of the holes over the five launchers positioned on either side of the center line. It was a bit of a bore after a while. There were no game features except launching the ball.

The football game was a monument to a different age. It consisted of a box whose top was a piece of glass. Inside was a 40-watt light bulb, which was powered by plugging a cord into an electrical outlet. One player took defense and the other offense. Each player had a set of transparencies with the play formations. These were matched up, laid on the glass and the bulb was turned on to show the results of the play. As soon as the offensive thrust (marked by a line) touched a defender, that was a tackle and the play was over. If no defender got in the way, touchdown!

It was great fun to try to outguess your opponent with play selection, but over time it became apparent the game had some serious shortcomings. Unlike the battery powered games of today, small children were plugging something into a wall outlet. As the game went on, the glass could get hot, not a good thing since the box itself was just pasteboard (and not so good for our fingers either). But most importantly, there was a fatal design flaw. We eventually discovered one of the offensive plays was unstoppable by any defense. It was virtually a guaranteed touchdown, which took the suspense out of the game, as we sat there and traded scores. It never occurred to us we could have solved this problem by pulling that play.

At some point, we both received some of the Steiff brand plush animals. We particularly liked the miniature versions and collected bears, monkeys, and all manner of bestiary. Each critter came with a name on a tag (which we might or might not adapt for our friend) and a steel button with the Steff logo in one of its ears. Thanks to the small sizes there were all sorts of wonderful things one could do. The bears could ride the zebra, the camel or the giraffe. Our little zoo offered all sorts of creative possibilities. Things like cereal boxes, oatmeal containers and (horrors!) cigarette cartons could be shaped into castles, airplanes, barns and other accommodations for our pals. Saran wrap was unknown but the cellophane from cigarette packages was quite suitable for windows.

While I was in grade school, marbles suddenly became quite popular, but more as a matter of collecting than playing the game. Few of us knew how to play marbles, let alone the technique of shooting a marble with a thumb, but the craze took off anyhow. People bought their bags of marbles to school to show off their steelies, cat-eyes, "glassies" or agates. Trades occasionally took place. It was an interest shared equally by the boys and the girls, and such common interests were rare in the 1950s. My wife still has a box of her marbles, which are very handy for arranging and anchoring artificial flowers.

Over the years there has been much controversy concerning children and toy weapons. In the 1950s by contrast, there were no qualms about arming small boys with rifles and six-shooters, and as illustrated in this volume, Jon and I were armed and dangerous (at least in our minds). Playing cowboys and robbers was a favorite past time occupying many hours on nice (and not so nice) days when we could go outside. Other friends introduced us to playing army, but fighting the Commies was never as much fun as chasing Jesse James. Over the years we also had pirate cutlasses, rubber Bowie knives, medieval swords and other instruments of mayhem but never much in the way of modern weaponry.

This was not the case if the conflict was to be acted out with toy soldiers. We had large armies of GI's complete with tanks, trucks, and artillery ready to take on all the enemies of our country. Thanks to the wonders of plastic injection molding, we could acquire our battalions at a reasonable cost. Thirty-nine cents would put a platoon in your hands, while if you wanted one of those nice diecast, hand-painted metal figures on sale at Woolworth's, you needed a dime per soldier. Accordingly, we bought just a few of the fancy models and designated them as our generals.

Over time, our ability to stage conflict was expanded to cowboys and Indians, the cavalry, medieval knights and the Civil War, though I won't try to pretend all this paraphernalia expanded our knowledge of history or military strategy. It was a great way to spend a Saturday afternoon when it was too cold or too rainy to go outside.

All sorts of products had offers for toys and novelties by mail order: "Yours for only 25c and two box tops!" Our principal sources for things we yearned to have were cereal box offers and comic book advertising. Over the years we ordered all sorts of stuff, most of which was terribly disappointing. The item often turned out to be a lot less special than advertised, flimsy, or inoperable. Our mother's grave warnings about the likely outcome always fell on deaf ears.

We were quite pleased, though, with our deeds to ¼ square inch of real estate in Alaska (thanks to the Sergeant Preston radio show), which was ours for something like 10 cents (which in those days were paid in postage stamps for ease of mailing). Another big favorite was the magic nuclear submarine, a plastic gizmo about 2 inches long with a secret compartment for "atomic fuel." When fueled and submerged in water, the submarine began to bubble and rose to the surface. It worked well but we quickly exhausted the little bag of white powder (the atomic fuel) that came with the boat. Tears were forestalled when Mother gave us some baking powder and it proved to be the secret ingredient.

Most of our toys, like our much-lamented baseball cards, disappeared in mysterious ways as time went on. Our frequent moves served to thin out our treasures as Mother struggled to get the household possessions pared down before we moved on to the next stop. We often gave our toys to younger neighbors when it became apparent we had outgrown them.

The toy soldiers ended up having a second and then a third act. Shortly after I entered Knox College the family was moving yet again, and our mother put me in charge of dealing with some toys still on hand. Among them was the large collection of toy soldiers. I packed them up and sent them to my cousin Craig, then about four years old. Then a few years ago, Craig was clearing out the attic in his parents' home and came across the soldiers. He sent them to my grandson, and after more than fifty years, I got to play with my army again.

Remembering Our Parents

Both parents exerted a powerful influence over our lives from the very first. They accomplished this without resorting to force, humiliation, domineering or any of the other ugly traits sometimes cited by people remembering forceful parents. Each of them exuded an authority that commanded our attention and did not admit of doubts. Eventually, we both revolted, but it was much later and not during the time span of this book.

We had distinctly different relationships with each parent. Since our father was absent for long periods of time throughout our childhood, he was an occasional figure, whereas our mother was a daily presence. She did not hesitate to invoke his authority when making her rulings, and so there was a virtual presence if not a physical one. It sometimes occurred to me to wonder how she could be so confident of his opinion (since he was at that moment in Baghdad, some 6400 miles away), but the issue was not open for discussion.

Dad concentrated almost entirely on his career. In his view, that was his duty, both to his family and to his talents. Although he was pleased with his financial success, money was not his only motive. He took pride in the technical accomplishments of his projects and his leadership skills. If he ever doubted himself, I never caught a glimpse of it. He had that self-confidence competent people possess. Whatever the problem, he was always confident he could identify what was going wrong and find a solution to address it.

Nelle had two guiding aims in life—to take care of her family and to be of service. Though she was devoted to her various community projects, family came first. She was as firmly committed to her husband's star as he, and willingly carried the load at home while he was overseas. There was always a curious anomaly in our mother's behavior. She was perfectly ready to defer to him on just about any issue. However, I would be hard pressed to think of anyone else who got the same treatment. Like our father, she had leadership and organizational skills and in the style of the day, put them to work at the PTA and other worthy causes. Where she might have ended up professionally had she been born a generation later can only be imagined.

Their personal styles were almost opposites in some respects. Unlike our father, our mother was a worrier at times, though she never let it get the better of her for very long. As our mentor and guide in matters of conduct and ethics, she sometimes lapsed into lecture mode. Dad's approach was more concise. His essential message went along these lines, "You know how we do things around here." Both were rule-oriented in their approach to moral questions. Situational ethics were not their style. Mother, despite being often more rigid in her mores than Dad, was the more inclined to make allowances for human foibles. Alfred Bourgo could be quite unforgiving, particularly in matters where he felt that the transgressor had not exercised self-control. He appeared to have almost perfect self-discipline and like many capable and focused people he was offended by poor judgment, sloppy workmanship, and cutting corners.

Both of our elders were endowed with considerable manual skills, which sadly, I did not inherit. Our mother was handy with a needle and made many lovely crocheted and needlepoint pictures (some of which still hang in our homes). Dad was an expert model maker and took on the kits that came with a set of plans, a few pieces of balsa and required a set of X-acto knives. Another of his skills was exquisite penmanship and the ability to write out block letters in perfect slant gothic. When later in life he discovered that engineering students were no longer expected to learn how to letter or even worse—how to draft—he was not pleased. It was akin to an artist who could not draw.

Our parents had different approaches to other people. Mother was warm and gregarious, the sort of person who could make a new friend during an elevator ride. From the many contacts she made in her various callings she assembled an enormous circle of pals. Our father, on the other hand, was a much more reserved and distant person. At times he appeared to have no need for close human contact other than his wife and children. Still, as we discovered after his death, he had many cordial professional relationships and those people described him as an exceedingly helpful and loyal friend. We were amazed to learn he was by common consent the lay chaplain of Harza Engineering.

There were still other differences. Our mother was a straightforward and open soul. There was never much mystery as to where her feelings lay. Although she enjoyed a joke (never risqué, of course!) humor was not her forte. She did not engage in kidding or banter to any great degree. Dad was much more oblique and often reserved his opinions. He was a great kidder and had an uncanny ability to pick up on the quirks and tics of the people he was around. He would deliberately downplay matters he really cared about (but didn't care to discuss) by deeming them silly or absurd. For example, he fended off inquiries about his boyhood by dismissing his family as a bunch of Joliet "micks."

Our father had a sincere love for great art, especially painting, and he acquired a large collection of beautifully illustrated books of reproductions. As we grew up, he took care to make sure that Jon and I appreciated the importance of the great figures in the visual arts. When I became interested in classical music in high school, he encouraged my enthusiasm by providing our home with some excellent recordings. Nelle, on the other hand, was not terribly drawn to the high culture of fine arts and classical music. She did believe that an understanding of such matters was being part of educated and she always supported our interests as we grew older.

Our mother was a typical Quaker in her outlook. She was not in the least interested in the theology and sacraments of orthodox Christianity. She was certain there was a God (likely what the Quakers call the inner light), but I doubt she had any use for the details of the Nicene Creed. Her faith was something she expressed in her outlook on life and in leading a life of service. Our father was a much more serious student of his beliefs and enjoyed reading religious authors such as Thomas Merton. He was at home among the liturgies and ceremonies of the Episcopal Church (which he attended as a boy), and over time he was drawn to the Catholic Church (which he increasingly attended when he was overseas).

They presented quite a contrast, this pair. Mother was largely intuitive and trusted her instincts. Dad was much more inclined to look at the details (he was after all an engineer). But it all worked out quite well over the years. They were married for 39 years and had few serious disagreements. I have always thought they were a good example of several observations one might make about successful unions. One, they complemented each other in many aspects, or as the old saw has it, "Opposites attract." The other, which I concede is unsatisfactory and unscientific, is that it's all a mystery. People who genuinely love and care for each other find their way around the details.

Passport photo of our father from the early 1950s

157

Summer Camp

Our parents were enthusiastic about summer camp. There were at least three reasons for their feelings. They never had such opportunities themselves, and in the time-honored style of parents, they wanted their children to have a better life. Secondly, I think they wanted us to be doing something constructive during the summer as opposed to sitting around the house. Thirdly, I suspect they didn't mind a break from parenting. Not all our camp experiences were as edifying as promised, but we did learn a few useful things and our memories of those days are mostly on the credit side of the ledger.

Being the oldest, I was the first to be dispatched to the great outdoors. My first venture was a day camp run by the local YMCA. We gathered each morning and a school bus hauled us out to a local forest preserve a few miles west of town. Going and coming we were led in song by an overenthusiastic counselor. Some of the songs (like "John Jacob Dingleheimerschmidt") sounded just plain silly, even to my eight-year-old ears. Still, every boy is happy to learn "A Hundred Bottles of Beer on the Wall."

I do not recall much of what we did there. There were crafts, fishing (we had our best results in an old swimming pool which had been flooded years before and never restored), and team sports (though not baseball, which I would have preferred). The last day we engaged in some sort of elaborate war game, which most of the younger campers, including me, found confusing, and which today seems plainly bizarre. Those were the years of the Cold War and many Americans were concerned about whether the younger generation would be up to the job of defeating the Commies. I would have given such people great concern. I was captured within a few minutes of the start and spent the afternoon sitting at the picnic table designated as the jail.

Several years later, I was dispatched to Boy Scout camp in Benton Harbor, Michigan, which was some 120 miles distant. The session lasted ten days, and my memories of this experience are not very positive. There was a fair amount of hazing, which was tolerated by our leaders as situation normal. The staff ran the place on a semi-military basis, and I got in trouble on several occasions for failing at some assigned duty. One involved my failure to get a fire going in a pot belly stove that heated water for the showers, and since building a fire was a hallowed Scout skill, it was a real humiliation.

Whatever my experience at camp, I thoroughly enjoyed being a member of BSA Troop 15, which met at our church every Monday evening. We were not a rowdy group, but ambition was not one of our hallmarks. Other troops were full of eager beavers intent on moving up the ranks to Eagle Scout, but not ours. I was a typical underachiever: I quickly moved up from Tenderfoot to Second Class my first year and then did little for two years. Our leader, a fatherly fellow, did not hide his disappointment at my sloth, but he was kind enough not to dwell on the matter.

What we all loved were the occasional weekends during the fall and spring at our nearby Scout campgrounds: Camp Ka-de-ka. Pitching tents, building fires, and cooking outdoors were all great fun. It was an adventure to walk through the woods hunting for firewood, tossing rocks in the creek and playing variations of hide and seek. We even tried to pay attention when our leaders insisted we work on skills such as tying knots, using a compass, marking a trail or reading maps. Saturday night was always eagerly awaited since we could stay up as late as we wanted—provided we were in our tents by the curfew. This was quite practical since by that time we had exhausted the batteries in our flashlights and would have quickly gotten lost in the dark. Despite the Scout motto none of us ever bothered to bring spares.

In 1958, now thirteen, I went back to Scout camp in Michigan, this time with much more success. I was thirteen and knew the ropes. Mysteriously enough that spring, I had suddenly acquired a burst of ambition and had finally finished my First-Class requirements and part of the merit badges I needed to rise to Star Scout. While at camp I worked hard to meet the remaining qualifications. However, after achieving that rank, I went back to my old ways and never added another badge to my sash.

I don't remember this fellow's name, but the picture came about because everyone in Scouts was convinced we could be twins.
You can see I am in full regalia with the merit badge sash and other trappings of my exalted rank. From summer 1958.

In the year between my two sojourns at scout camp, it was decided I should attend the national Scout Jamboree at Valley Forge. Our scouting council picked one of the more enthusiastic scoutmasters in town to head our delegation to the Jamboree. He wanted to lead a smart unit and drilled us endlessly in marching. For some of the programs at the event, he planned elaborate demonstrations of skills which required lengthy rehearsals. This was all much in contrast with the casual atmosphere of Troop 15.

I was the only scout from my troop who went and the youngest boy of the forty or so who made the trip from Aurora. Luckily for me, a few of the older boys were happy to have an adoring acolyte, and their kindly attentions made the experience a positive one. At the Jamboree, I had the honor—dubious in retrospect—of shaking hands with Richard M. Nixon, and even though I was a Democrat, I was quite thrilled. On the way home from the gathering we went to Washington DC for some sightseeing and I had the pleasure of getting to see my Uncle Neil and Aunt Edna.

With one of my heroes, about to take off for the Jamboree in 1957. We are standing at the Burlington station in downtown Aurora.

My brother followed my lead and did several summers in the Y day camp, where his favorite memory was a field trip to the Mars candy factory. In the summer of 1958, when he was ten, he was dispatched for six weeks to Camp Ney-a-Ti, a classic summer camp—sports, fishing, swimming lessons, crafts, and nature study, all accompanied by various and sundry mystic rituals allegedly modeled after the practices of Native Americans and Hawaiians. We took it for authentic and thoroughly enjoyed the experience. I joined him for the second three weeks after scout camp and for the next two years, we went together for six weeks each summer.

Ney-a-Ti was a democratic experience. The cost was modest and the campers were mostly from the broad middle of American society. We were all expected to take our turns helping to bus tables in the dining room, clean the bathhouse and police the grounds. Everybody had to make his bed and keep his clothes tucked away. Each morning our bunkhouse had to pass inspection before we could move into the day's program.

Camp Ney-a-Ti, probably the summer of 1959. Neither Jon nor I can recall the name of our companion, but we are both sure he was one of the best athletes that year.

The camp was located on the site of an old resort on Summit Lake, not far from the Wisconsin border with the Upper Peninsula. It was run by the McKenzie family (mother, father, and son) who were athletic coaches and PE teachers at Northern Illinois University. Mrs. Mac ran the dining room, led singalongs and taught crafts. Mr. Mac was not able to leave his job for the entire summer and was only occasionally on hand. When he was around, it was a treat, as we looked on him as that wise and kindly grandfather every boy wanted to have. Their son, Jim, was the sports director and organizer of many of the special activities. Jim was a kind man, an excellent athlete, and knew a great deal about a great many subjects. Most of the campers (including my brother and I) idolized him.

In addition to our daily routines we had special events like a track meet, plays, a Christmas party, a gold rush (we all hunted for painted rocks that had been scattered around the property—while the counselors played robbers) and glorious mass games of "kick the can." Older boys got to take an overnight canoe trip and there would be occasional outings to the Paul Bunyan Museum and other local attractions. If it rained, we all gathered in the dining hall for bingo games or other activities Mrs. Mac had for such occasions.

The Macs also understood how to motivate us to do our best. At the end of the session, everyone received a plywood plaque shaped like a shield with the names of 12 or 15 categories stenciled in three columns. Some pertained to skills like swimming or boating, some to participation (acting in a play), and others to citizenship and good behavior. If you qualified in a category, a colored ribbon was affixed in the appropriate space with a thumbtack. Campers who came back for additional years could have the thrill of watching the tacks change colors from blue to silver to gold. My brother and I worked hard at getting every space filled and eventually we both managed to achieve our goal of 100%.

There were always a few disagreeable kids, and one summer, a decidedly unpleasant counselor—a former marine who thought he was still part of the Corps. I suppose such encounters were in part what our parents had in mind. Not all experiences are perfect, but they won't last forever, either. Sometimes, we just have to wait it out until things change, as inevitably they will. The following year, that counselor was not re-hired and the normal collection of jerks at least had different faces.　That is the one good thing I can recall about the stinkers: they rarely came back for a second year.

Boy Scout Troop 15 (1957)

We often failed our campsite inspection,
were always found out of uniform,
and were mostly stuck at the lower ranks,
lacking that essential Scout knowledge
of knots, Indian lore, and Morse code,
easily one of the worst troops in the Council,
but we liked spending time with each other.

Once in a while by some misadventure,
we might recruit an ambitious fellow,
anxious to wrap up the First-Class badge
and start working towards Eagle,
but he would invariably leave us
for one of the well-turned-out units
picked to march in the Labor Day parade.

What kept us in the band was fun,
those weekends together in the woods
away from curious parents,
the absolute joy of starting a fire,
tossing rocks into the creek,
and staying up as late as we could,
spurred on by dirty jokes and ghost stories.

The value of our learning was debatable,
and our characters did not visibly improve;
no doubt we could have been guided
to better uses of our time and energy,
but at that age the accounts were infinite,
and our leader was a kind and patient man
who clearly knew that soon enough,
we'd be adults for the rest of our lives.

The Kingbird

In 1955 when I was ten,
birds acquired a magic:
so many names to learn,
colors and shapes to master,
a panorama of beings
I had scarcely conceived.
From my fifth-grade teacher,
I learned that knowing the birds
was an honorable pursuit,
that we were obligated
to recognize those creatures
with whom we shared the earth,
that learning the names
was an offering of respect.

Armed with my Peterson's Guide
I traveled the neighborhood
(a bird haven just four blocks
from downtown Aurora, Illinois),
recording my discoveries
in the margins of the book.
Reading the entries today,
written in clear childish strokes,
many finds were quite likely:
January 22, I noted a cardinal,
two days hence an English Sparrow,
and later that spring, a robin.
Some were merely implausible—
a Chipping Sparrow on April 5—
and others purely impossible:
for example, my April 20 report
of a Western (or Arkansas) Kingbird,
a species rarely tempted
to venture much east of Omaha.
Along with companion sightings
of equal improbability,

here was the paper trail of my sin,
claiming birds I could not have seen,
tempted into false witness
by the hope of a phoenix,
ambition and enthusiasm
displacing well-earned modesty.

Thanks to Mr. Williams,
birds have been a lifetime habit,
a faith outlasting many others,
and so on August 16, 2005,
I got— at last— a clear view
of *Tyrannus Verticalis,*
the Western Kingbird itself,
perched in a low tree
and reigning over his field
just east of Pullman, Washington.
The imagined had become real
and after a half-century
a record has been squared—
but I still need to find
a European Tree Sparrow.

Amusements and Favorite Things

As I start this chapter it is almost July 4, which reminded me of one of our favorite summertime activities—catching lightning bugs. Around Aurora, the peak of the season normally coincided with the holiday and lasted only a few weeks. Nothing topped the pleasure of being able to go outside after dark—therefore after bedtime—and chase after the flashing dots of light in the summer air. They flew slowly and were easy to catch. We carried old mayonnaise jars or other containers (imagine the horror of today's cautious parents— children running around holding glass bottles!) with holes punched in the lids to put our treasures in. Sooner or later someone would call us in. We'd count our haul and then, as instructed by our mother, release them to fly off and do whatever lightning bugs do— until the next time we caught them.

Another pleasure of summertime was roller skates. Though I know there were roller rinks when we were growing up, I was then unaware that skating could be done indoors. Our skates were a heavy metal arrangement which attached to the shoes with a set of clamps. Tightening and untightening the clamps required a key, a hex wrench that turned the bolts. Predictably enough, the key was often lost or misplaced. In this case, a guy had to hope somebody with a key might be out on skates. This was often a girl: as anyone could tell you, they were more responsible, and they had no objection to wearing their key on a string around their neck. For us boys that was too close to jewelry.

Skating must have been a great boon for the makers of Band-Aids and Mercurochrome. There were always uneven spots in the sidewalk that were treacherous to navigate—not to speak of the general problem which I often experienced—a fundamental lack of grace and athletic skills. Concrete is an unforgiving surface and our elbows and knees regularly advertised our unplanned encounters with pavement. (If you are wondering about Mercurochrome, it was a once widely used over-the-counter antiseptic banned by the FDA in 1998. It did indeed contain mercury.)

Another significant mode of transportation was a bicycle. There were two essential issues. First, you needed to know how to ride. The second was to own one. Much about bicycles in our era was different. Bicycle helmets did not exist and no one worried about riding around without safety equipment. The small sizes available today that allow six-year-olds to ride two-wheelers were not readily available. The only alternate size wasn't much smaller than the standard model. That combined with parental attitudes about the age of responsibility meant many of us had to wait quite a time before we acquired a set of wheels we could call our own. I was perhaps in the summer between fifth and sixth grade, but my brother (always the beneficiary of my pathfinding as the elder sibling) did not have to wait quite so long.

Thanks to the tutelage of an older neighbor boy named Lyle, I learned to ride well before I owned a bike. Lyle was a bicycle genius, a fellow we admired much as we would later admire the guy in high school who took cars apart and put them back together again. He was always tinkering with his bike and adding improvements like electric lights, horns, fancy seats and the like. He converted an old standard bike to a sporty model with three speeds and fancy handlebars. Upon discovering I did not know how to ride, he took matters in hand and I surprised myself by learning quickly.

Our mother, unfortunately, was not impressed by my new prowess. She warned me constantly about the responsibility of riding borrowed equipment and severely limited my sphere of activity—I was confined to the sidewalk. Though I am sure I thought I had to wait forever, it probably wasn't more than a year and I finally had a bicycle of my own to ride, and with it the liberty to ride in the street though with certain limitations. My bicycle was a Schwinn middleweight, a compromise between English racers and the fat tire models popular in the US. It did not have three speeds or handbrakes, but it was speedier than the tank varieties.

For some reason, my brother had trouble learning how to ride. It must be one of the few tests of athletics or physical dexterity that ever proved difficult for him. Unlike me, he had a bike before he learned how to ride. One Saturday morning our father and I took him over to the Catholic school playground and all at once, he got the idea and took off. There was now no stopping the boy, and we were soon riding bikes when we went over to the Todd playground to look for a ball game. I know this episode must have been in the spring of 1957, for we had just gotten a new Scottie pup (Carol) and she was with us on this expedition.

Carol was our second dog. Our first dog, Keynote, was not at all child-oriented. Like most dogs, he was adept at sorting out the family hierarchy, and he decided he was higher on the scale than the children. Though he would consent to chase a ball we had thrown and would deign to accept a treat from us, he was not our dog. Carol was only a few months old when she arrived, and Jon and I were already old enough to be involved in various aspects of dog care. As a result, she was much more of a pal and enjoyed our attention. She even obeyed us when it took her fancy.

Our girl was a real exemplar of the Scottie character. She did not care for other dogs and made no secret of her feelings. Larger dogs did not cow her in the least. She was also an accomplished hunter of small animals and birds. By contrast, Keynote was enthusiastic but ineffective. Carol not only gave chase, but she also nabbed the quarry occasionally. When guests or strangers came to the house, she was polite but not solicitous. Being our dog was more than enough for her. Sadly enough, she died prematurely at six and was genuinely mourned.

Then as now, Halloween was a high point of the year. The return to school in September was the launch point for thinking about Halloween and making the tough decisions about what sort of costume you wanted. Our mother was handy with a needle in many ways, but it did not extend to our Halloween costumes. As far as she was concerned, that was a job for Woolworth's, and this bothered us not at all. In our later years, Jon and I may have tried to be a little more creative, but in early childhood, the getup was out of a box. Once again, safety standards were rather lax: one year it rained, and the red dye in my brother's costume ran. His face was stained for days before it finally faded.

We wore our costumes to school on the big day and had a party. At some point in the upper grades, we stopped wearing our outfits but there were still treats at the end of the school day. I probably went out on the hunt for the last time about eighth grade. My brother thus had to manage on his own, and by then we had also moved to a new neighborhood where the fun was no longer quite the same.

I am sure there must have been a few years when I was escorted by a parent, but by third grade or so, I was on my own and charged with keeping an eye on Jon. It was great fun going up and down the street stopping at every house to get our candy. Older siblings were often along to keep an eye on things and accepted the offerings with feigned reluctance. Over the years we came to know the identity of the generous souls and the cheapskates. We also knew some places might be profitable (for example, the Copley mansion) but possibly inconvenient. If the eccentric Mrs. Copley answered the door, she might demand that we do a trick for her. I recall one year when I whistled a song for her and she promptly requested an encore. Eventually, we did get out but it was a considerable effort, even for a full-sized nickel candy bar.

The Catholic convent near the school was a great stop in terms of the haul but again, an investment of time. The sister who greeted us at the door proceeded to take us on a lengthy tour of the house so all the nuns could see us and say hello. There would also be various questions about what you liked to do, what grade you were in and where you lived. That five minutes or so felt like forever, but they were so nice to us that it was hardly right to be annoyed.

It was always good to find a few friends along the way and form a sizeable posse for the hunt. Halloween was not a quiet evening, as the sidewalks filled noisy children dashing from porch to porch. There would often be a few kids from some other street joining us, people we did not know, and whatever social distance might have been usual was lost in the enthusiasm we all felt for this sheer enjoyment. A few parents always tried to guess who was at their door and there was nothing quite as satisfying as feeling you had really flummoxed someone who otherwise knew who you were. It never occurred to us they were playing along, as we were sure that our disguises were fool-proof.

Over the years, as we were permitted to stay out later, we managed to expand the boundaries to include more and more territory. The quantities of candy seemed vast to us. Once home, we poured it out and started to sort it out—candy bars, suckers, bubble gum and so forth. Homemade goodies like popcorn balls, fudge, and cookies were accepted and consumed without concern. We reveled in our favorites like Snickers and Hershey bars and wondered if this might be the year we finally liked Butterfingers. We soon started to consume our treasures, no matter what good intentions we might have uttered about parceling them out carefully. Some years we even managed to make the stuff last a whole week, though we were never desperate enough to eat the licorice.

Church, Campbell, and Haircuts

Not long after we moved to Aurora, our parents decided their sons would be pagans no more and set about finding a place to send them to Sunday school. They settled on Our Savior Lutheran Church, conveniently located on the other side of the street. Our Savior was a compromise of sorts: it was liturgical enough to suit our Catholic leaning father and at least nominally Protestant, which mattered to our Quaker mother.

I recall Jon and I attended Sunday school for a while before the parents started attending Sunday morning services. Unlike some churches, the Lutherans thought that all children should attend both church and Sunday school. Church services took place at eight and ten-thirty; Sunday school was at 9:15. So for many years, we were rolled out early on Sundays as our parents preferred to attend the early service.

At some point, it dawned upon Mother and Dad that my little brother was at risk of his mortal soul. He had never been baptized and this omission needed to be addressed. By now he was five or so and old enough to participate in the planning. When the question of godparents came up he had clear wishes. He wanted Mr. Feltz to be his godfather. Mr. Feltz was a terribly nice man and an indefatigable church volunteer. Every Sunday morning he stood at the curb outside the church directing traffic and shepherding children safely out of their cars and into the parsonage where Sunday school was held. In our case, it was his mission to get us safely across Downer Place. Jon had taken quite a fancy to him and that settled the matter. Al and Nelle invited Mr. and Mrs. Feltz to sponsor him, which they were happy to do. Many years later Mr. Feltz made a special effort to come to our father's funeral, explaining to Jon that he was merely doing his duty as a godparent.

Jon and I have similar memories of our Bible lessons from the early days. The Old Testament was clearly our favorite. It had all the good stories and all the neat heroes like David, Joshua, and Gideon.

Nothing stirs hearts quite like war, murder, and sex, and the Old Testament had a generous helping of them all. I do suspect our teachers did not dwell on such matters as David's interest in Bathsheba or the hit job he did on Uriah the Hittite—nor did they linger over Abraham's various peccadillos with Hagar the Egyptian.

At age four or five, my brother was particularly taken with the story of the fiery furnace in the book of Daniel, and our father was much amused with Jon's recital. He would invite Jon to tell him the story, and as Jon got to the end of his narration, Dad would cue him to say the names of the three heroes. Jon would duly respond by piping in his loudest voice, "Shad-rack, Me-sack, and Abend-dee-go!"

By contrast, the New Testament was dull stuff. A few of Jesus's miracles were intriguing but for the most part, I found Jesus to be somewhat incomprehensible. How could it be that a guy with super powers let everybody knock him around like that? In truth, he was a little like the Lone Ranger's faithful Indian companion Tonto, a patsy who was always drawing the short straw. Some of his advice made no sense. Even at nine, I was pretty sure the meek not would inherit the earth.

Heading up this enterprise was an energetic and likable man, Pastor Paul Krentz. It was thanks to his influence and charisma my parents started attending services not too long after we had joined the Sunday School. Our Savior was Missouri Synod Lutheran, a rigid and conservative bunch, but our church was part of something called the English District—both an effort to evangelize among the unchurched, and a mission to appeal to people outside the traditional ethnic bounds of Lutheranism. As such, the tone at Our Savior was more relaxed than at the other Lutheran parishes in town, which still had German language worship. Pastor Krentz was an excellent preacher and uninclined to press for public confessions of faith. I am sure this was appreciated by both Al and Nelle since both thought overt declarations of religious faith were in bad taste.

As time went on, Paul Krentz became a family friend as well as our pastor. He enjoyed visiting with our parents because they were entirely unselfconscious around him. They allowed him to relax and take off his collar, a privilege he would not have been able to assume with most of his flock. He and our father enjoyed their conversations, which roamed over many topics, and Dad always had a bottle of Munich Kummel in the liquor cabinet for the pastor to enjoy. Occasionally, Jon and I were guests at the parsonage and enjoyed playing Triominoes and other games left behind by the Krentz children, who were largely grown and gone by this point. Mrs. Krentz was a skilled artist and did portraits of us in pastels. Both Jon and I worshiped their college-age son, Pete, who was the epitome of a real guy—smart, clever and athletic—but were crushed when he succumbed to some girl and got married.

Eventually, it was time to get serious about the articles of faith. At the age of twelve, I was enrolled in catechism class which met once a week on Wednesday afternoons. It lasted for two years and the curriculum was straightforward. We went through Luther's *Small Catechism* from beginning to end the first year and in the second year, we repeated the whole process. In effect, we were expected to be able to regurgitate the contents of the book upon command. Pastor Paul was a very firm teacher. Homework assignments such as Bible readings, sermon notes, and matters to be memorized (the creeds, the Ten Commandments, etc.) were to be done as prescribed. Slackers were put on notice that confirmation was in no way an automatic process—unlike milk and water Protestants, a Lutheran had to earn his place at the communion rail by demonstrating he had the whole story down pat.

In later years I have wondered how much of this draconian regime of rote learning was due to Krentz. As I learned in my later years, after I had been in college a while and acquired some knowledge of history and theology, Paul Krentz was a highly educated and sophisticated thinker whose notions were far subtler than most of his flock. I am certain some of this old-fashioned emphasis was due to his consideration of what the congregation expected of him. The vestry demanded a public examination of the catechumens before the confirmation ceremony took place. However, the pastor was no dummy when it came to such matters. The performance was carefully planned: we all knew which questions we were personally responsible for, and some of us were primed to volunteer so as to lend an air of spontaneity to the process.

My brother reminded me of another special Krentz touch to the exercise the year he was being confirmed. There was a boy in his class who was learning-disabled but Pastor Paul saw no reason not

Mike and Pastor Krentz on Confirmation Sunday, April 1958

to include him the process. This fellow was so pleased to get a question and to get the right answer that he just about popped the buttons on his surplice. Naturally, the answer was "Jesus."

Aside from matters theological, the church played a definite role in our social life, especially when Dad was out of town.   Nelle was lukewarm about Lutheranism, but she enjoyed the volunteer and the social outlets the church offered. We were enthusiastic participants in the various potluck meals, Easter Sunday breakfasts, and parish social hours. During Lent, there were additional events (devotionals of a sort) held in the parish hall where we got to watch episodes of the "Lutheran Hour," half-hour films that were also run on TV. Jon and I were very taken with these vignettes, which were along the lines of "Leave It to Beaver," but with an emphasis on messages that were explicitly religious as opposed to the anodyne moral tone of secular TV. The dramas featured the Fisher family, composed of a wise father, a caring mother and several kids who got into trouble either through bad decisions or evil companions. For variety, the troubled soul was by turns a family friend, fellow parishioner or neighbor. By some good fortune, there was a dad for guidance, a mom for emotional support, a kindly pastor who showed up as needed, and by the time twenty-five minutes had gone by, the miscreant was back on track and everybody had their smile pasted back on.

The church also sponsored various and sundry wholesome programs such as lectures and presentations by visiting missionaries and other worthies. Not all the offerings were strictly religious, and the one which appealed the most to Jon and me was the appearance of Sam Campbell, "The Philosopher of the Forest." Sam was variously an author, a filmmaker and a naturalist. He was an early proponent of environmental protection, though he was not a serious scientist or crusader along the lines of Aldo Leopold or Rachel Carson. Instead, Sam just wanted us to appreciate the outdoors and the wisdom which accrued to those who listened carefully to Nature. Here are a few quotations which give a taste of what he was about:

"There are few living things whose purpose in the great scheme cannot be clearly seen if we get rid of our fears and think wisely."

"One has sensed little of the real beauty of the natural world if he has not been moved to tears."

Sam's format never varied. The bulk of his presentation was a story about an animal which he delivered while showing a silent film which illustrated his narrative. He created characters from the animals he saw around his summer home in the North Woods and told us endearing tales of Loony Coon and Pepper the Porcupine. Such personifications today would be scorned, but we absolutely soaked the stuff up. Naturally, at the end of his performance, there was an opportunity to buy one of his books and learn more about all our special friends who lived in the woods.

Jon and I read at least a half dozen of his books and never gave a thought to the fact that a good deal of the narrative material was pure fiction. We were too wrapped up in Loony's close brush with a predatory owl or an evil coyote to wonder just how Sam knew all about those adventures in such minute detail. Over the years we went to several of Sam's events at various sites around town, but by the end, we were losing interest. Sam increasingly shifted his emphasis from Minnesota to Hawaii, and we found his travelogues of life in the islands considerably less interesting than stories about fetching little porcupines and resourceful raccoons.

To be a good and faithful Lutheran, a fellow needed to be properly groomed, so that will provide the transition to my discussion of another essential institution in our town: Ken's Barber Shop, where my brother and I got our hair cut throughout the years we lived in Aurora. Since our mother was a devotee of crew cuts for boys, we made frequent trips to Ken's. Her distaste for even slightly long hair did not seem reasonable to me. Our father wore his in a classic pompadour, long and brushed straight back. This was yet another illustration of the fact that she had a different rule book for the old man than for us. I was sixteen before I revolted, and I succeeded only on the pretext it was required for a play I was acting in at my high school.

Ken's was at the edge of the downtown area, across the street from Strathmore's (where the "Magic Slate" was manufactured) and just a few doors from the lurid mysteries of Ray's Spider Web. It was a perpetually busy place late in the afternoons and on Saturdays, which was when we were usually dispatched to get our hair cut. When very young, we got our hair cut by Dad, but his frequent absences meant Mother had to find another way to manage our coiffures. As it was an all-male enclave (no manicurists, thank you) I am sure she was relieved when we reached an age when we did not need her supervision.

Reservations were not accepted, and one was likely to spend more time waiting than getting served—especially the case if one was a youngster. Our haircuts were considerably discounted, and I doubt any barber spent more than ten minutes on a kid. There were frequently more patrons waiting than being shorn even though the shop usually had at least four barbers on duty. Fortunately, Ken had a large supply of sports magazines available for perusal. There may have been other publications for older customers, but they were not left out where younger eyes might find them.

The lack of reservations also meant that it was hit or miss in terms of the guy who cut your hair. Ken himself was cordial but businesslike and not interested in talking to children. Over the years we developed favorites, but we only got to climb into their chairs on an irregular basis. Naturally enough, there were also characters we did not care for at all. One fellow always gave me a hard time because I cheered for the White Sox and the Cardinals instead of the Cubs and the Bears. For a while, we even had to put up with a barber who professed to like the New York Yankees. It never occurred to me there was anything to talk about at the barber shop except sports. I knew for certain no one there was in the slightest bit interested in what I did at school. As we grew up, the barbers were less hesitant to let us overhear adult conversation such as their near-constant ribbing of their youngest colleague, alleged to be a ladies' man.

179

There was another side to Ken's which completely passed us by in our salad days. My brother, always a more astute observer than I, figured it out when he was in high school. One day he overheard a strange exchange between a patron and one of the barbers, and he realized they were using some sort of code to set up a wager. So, in addition to cutting hair, Ken's was also a front for a bookie operation that handled bets on sports. No doubt this was a service that many citizens found useful because in those days there were only two places to place a legal bet—at a horse track or in Las Vegas.

How the mighty can fall! At age eight I would never have imagined such a fine business had any connection to the underworld. Our father, a man with a tolerant view of such human frailties as gambling or a drink, would have just smiled and shaken his head. I doubt it would have bothered Nelle C. Bourgo a great deal, either. Though a woman with an acute sense of right and wrong, she was a practical soul. If no harm was being done to anyone, she would not have let it disturb her equanimity. On the other hand, I can only imagine her fury if they had left out the cheesecake where small boys could get a peek.

The Neighbors

After we arrived in Aurora, it was not long before we started meeting the neighbors. Our mother was sociable and took the initiative of making contacts. For Dad, it would have been more difficult since he commuted to Chicago. He was gone for the better portion of the day and had no working peers to interact with in Aurora. He always seemed to be the only Harza employee in town.

Neither parent was much interested in the country club, fraternal organizations or the like. Nelle found many friends in her volunteer and civic undertakings. Our father's circumstances were further limited by his frequent and lengthy absences overseas. I have concluded both found family life their preferred setting. They seemed perfectly happy to be at home most evenings.

The first friends I recall were the Doanes, who lived about half a block west of us on Downer Place. The Doane household was both congenial and casual. In contrast to our operation, things there did not seem quite as orderly and predictable. Our mother was certainly not as pristine or regimented as some homemakers, but things tended to follow a plan.

By contrast, life at the Doanes seemed a little haphazard. No doubt, the composition of the family contributed to this circumstance. Their four children were separated by some 12 years, the father, Ellis, commuted to Chicago and had somewhat irregular work hours, and the mother (Sally) had community interests, and in later years, a career of her own. All this meant there was a variety of schedules with lots of potential for conflicts. Sally cheerfully confessed she had little interest in housework, and regularly joked about her ad hoc approach to meals. She loved a party and one year her New Year's festivities were enlivened by a pink Christmas tree she found in the trash outside one of the local bars.

Her mother (Stevie) also lived with them, but Stevie, though well past retirement age, always had a job of her own and like her daughter, little interest in housekeeping. She had been a pioneering career woman who worked past 70 at NCR and reluctantly allowed herself to be retired. She could play the grande dame with verve and the Bourgos were all fond of her. To stave off boredom she managed the Hallmark store for a while, and Jon and I always dropped by to say hello when we were downtown. For many years she also presented the novelty of being the only adult we had ever met who insisted we call her by her first name.

The Doanes were a clan that always seemed to be having fun. The sole son, Terry, was a few years older than I and moved through life with the grace and confidence younger boys find so alluring in older fellows. We were thrilled if he chanced to join the neighborhood pack on the way to school in the morning. Whether true or not, it seemed to me that the Doane kids had fewer responsibilities than I did, and I was envious. In the end, it was not a bad thing for me, a soul always a bit too close to the rulebook, to learn that each family succeeds in its own fashion. Though being neat might have its rewards, it was not one of the cardinal virtues.

Jon and I were always happy to be invited to the Doanes for TV after school while our mothers sat in the kitchen drinking coffee and talking away. Nelle and Sally shared an affinity for Democratic politics, a strong bond in a town where the Democrats were lucky to attract a third of the vote. Although their personalities and styles differed, they both enjoyed their endless conversations. Sally loved it when one of Mother's chatty brothers or sisters happened to be in Aurora. Both women were both individualists who did not worry much about the opinion of others. Neither had much use for excess piety, propriety, or fussiness, and they both enjoyed a drink and a cigarette in an era when some people ostentatiously avoided both.

We rarely did anything special with the Doanes. Our relationship was largely a casual, drop-in sort of arrangement. I don't ever recall eating dinner at their home or entertaining them in ours, though a time or two we did go out to eat or on an expedition to Phillips Park for a picnic. Our father and Ellis had a more distant relationship than their wives, but they did the morning commute together for a while and Ellis would occasionally drop by for a drink with Dad.

The Doanes had a ping pong table in the garage and we were amazed when our old man jumped into a game one night and proved to be an excellent competitor. Dad was sedentary around the house and had never shown any athletic inclinations.

Eventually, we spent less time with the Doanes, because our third home in Aurora was much further away. Even as the two families drifted apart, though, we never lost touch with each other through the various moves my peripatetic parents made. During the years we were away at college, Christmas and holiday breaks almost always included a visit with the Doanes and some years later we dropped by one Sunday afternoon to introduce my new bride.

Other acquaintances sprang from people we met at school. The Scafes were another family we occasionally saw. There were four boys and one much younger girl in their family. Jon and I each had a classmate among the boys and were in school with them throughout our public-school years. Musical talent ran strong in this clan and at least three of the boys were excellent musicians. The mother was my Cub Scout den leader and I looked forward to our weekly meeting in the Scafe home. Martine always knew what things might be interesting for us to do, and she was so nice to us that I was always on my best behavior. She also worked with our mother in the PTA and on school elections

Like our father, Dennis Scafe, Sr. was an engineer, though he was associated with one of the local manufacturing outfits. He seemed ancient to me though he was likely not yet fifty. The Scafes were fond of vacation road trips and always owned one of the enormous station wagons of that era—they did need the space, after all. I can recall Bruce fuming one evening when we had dropped by. He had just acquired a new buggy which was getting seven mpg in town. In those days gas only cost 25 cents a gallon, but even so, he contended, Detroit was just a bunch of slackers who did not know how to produce a good piece of machinery.

The friend I most often visited in grade school was Lester C. Brewick, Jr., otherwise known as Chip, and he certainly did resemble his father. The Brewicks consisted of Rosemary and Bud, the parents, Chip and his younger sister and brother, who were twins. They lived close by and I could get to their house in less than ten minutes. From time to time, I went home with him after school. We might toss a baseball around, look over some new toys, watch TV (everyone had a TV except the Bourgos!) or enjoy the generous snacks provided by Rosemary. Chip and I were Cub Scouts together and proudly wore our uniforms at school on National Scouting Day.

My enduring memory of the Brewicks is that they were among the nicest people I ever met. Both Bud and Rosemary were caring and considerate in every way, and they certainly passed that trait on. Chip did not have a mean bone in his body. He was fond of kidding people and adept at picking up on those traits we might wish others would overlook, but he never hurt my feelings. With him, it was never mean but just good-natured fun.

Chip was my pal from beginning to end in the school years. In high school, we were both in a group of four or five boys who regularly did something together on Friday night because none of us had much luck in the dating department. If one of us was absent due to a rare date, that guy was in for a thorough ribbing the next time he joined up with the gang. In those days, high schoolers were less likely to have a car and Chip's ownership made him a much-envied soul. He was our regular chauffeur and at the end of the night out, everyone handed over a quarter for the gas.

A few years after we moved to 26 South Chestnut Street, we had new neighbors next door—Ed and Bobbie Kubisak. They had not been married much more than a couple of years and had a baby son named Jeff. Ed and Bobbie were another unlikely match, at least for those days. He was from one of the Polish enclaves on Chicago's north side and she was a Protestant suburban girl from Highland Park. I don't recall how they met, but Bobbie defied her disapproving parents and they eloped. By the time they moved to 24 South Chestnut, though, things had been patched up with her parents, who were frequent visitors. The arrival of grandchildren is often a big help.

Jeff Kubisak's second birthday party, April 1958. From left Mike, Bobbie (with Kenny in front) and Ed (standing behind Jeff).

Ed was in his mid-twenties but Bobbie was much younger—barely 20 or so when they arrived. Our mother took an immediate maternal interest in them and was always a sucker for babies. Jon and I were fascinated as they were the first young married people we got to know. At some point or the other when I was about 13, it was determined I was up to short babysitting stints. Aside from my brother, Jeff was the first baby I spent a lot of time with. Jon and I were regular visitors, and we always felt welcome there, though I suspect we must have been a nuisance at times. If so, it was never even hinted.

Their second son (Kenny) was born with a cleft palate. Ed and Bobbie went through all the traumas of continuous medical intervention with a determination and grit we Bourgos found quite admirable. It was difficult to feed Kenny and he was subject to constant infections. Happily enough, newer surgical techniques promised real solutions, and after multiple procedures, little Kenny was able to lead a normal life and was soon thriving.

Ed had an office job and was going to night school. Like many children of immigrants, he was ambitious to find a career which involved his brains more than his hands. When Caterpillar opened a large plant near Aurora, he got a job there in purchasing and many years later retired as assistant director. On several occasions, I happened to see Ed working on his homework from night school, and I was amazed to see him writing it out with a ballpoint pen. At my school, we were still at the stage of a first draft in pencil before entrusting our work to the finality of ink. Evidently, Ed was less concerned he would need to erase anything.

The Kubisaks also differed greatly in their personalities. Ed was calm, on the quiet side and never seemed to lose his temper or his equilibrium. Bobbie was opinionated, talkative and could be hot-tempered. At age 13 and 14, I genuinely appreciated her interest in me. She was one of the first adults who talked to me as a peer and who offered me some welcome sympathy and counsel as I struggled through the eighth grade. Being only a few years older than I was, she had more sympathy for my struggles with puberty than our parents did. On several occasions, she got irked with my caution and timidity and encouraged me to be a more venturesome soul. That was a hopeless project. It was many years before I finally managed a measure of social aplomb.

This chapter came to an end when we moved on to new quarters in a distant neighborhood in the fall of 1959. At some point, in 2004 or so, I heard from Bobbie again. She had found some old 8mm movie film she had gotten from our mother and never returned (it turned out to be a film record of one of Nelle's pet projects—outdoor education—on its maiden launch). Thanks to the Internet she had tracked me down in Iowa and thereafter we stayed in touch until she died in 2009. Ed followed not long after in 2012. In later years (after raising five children) they had moved to New Mexico and become hot air ballooning enthusiasts.

Mike and Kenny Kubisak 1958

As I have often noted, Al and Nelle followed their own drummer in life. One of the things that did not attract them was the business of entertaining people in their home. I am hard pressed to think of more than a time or two when we had someone in for dinner. Aside from the annual Christmas bash for her political allies, Mother was not interested in offering parties. Even our birthday parties were usually a matter of inviting a good friend or two out for lunch and a movie. Their entertaining was mostly spur of the moment—the pastor dropping in for an after-dinner visit and a liqueur, a neighbor sharing a gin and tonic on the front porch with Dad, or Mother serving up coffee to a friend who appeared at the front door.

I suppose their other outlets (our mother's volunteer activities and our father's occupation, including the many people he knew overseas) supplied much of their need for a social life. Of course, these aspects of their lives were a mystery to me when I was growing up, and it was not until I was much older that I started to get a few insights into what exceptional and capable souls they were. I suppose it much the same for many of us: when young, our parents were so thoroughly assigned to the categories of Mom and Dad that many aspects of their lives as individuals simply went unseen.

26 South Chestnut Street (Summer 1956)

The house was a four-square from 1892
built on a small lot near downtown,
with a large front porch shaded by elms,
and the old barn still standing at the rear,
all of which left precious little space
for the game of games, baseball,
which was how we spent that summer.

It was a special home for our mother,
the first she could decorate as her own,
but to us mostly a place to eat and sleep,
a stop between our many innings
either playing catch on the sidewalk,
or improvising two-man games in the rear,
putting many windows in harm's way.

Each day included cornflakes, peanut butter,
the box scores in the *Tribune,*
and a trip to the schoolyard to join
long games of work-up, five hundred,
pitcher's hand out or second base over,
any form that could fill the geometry,
send a ball over the diamond into space.

After dinner as the day was ending,
we'd have a final game of catch,
and in bed in the darkening room
we might be granted a few innings
of our Chicago White Sox on the radio,
soon almost asleep as the voice droned on;
and finally, a good night from our father,
the last sound on a warm August night.

Baseball

I am not sure there are words or means to express the importance of this game in our childhood. It was an interest (we studied its history and statistics), a passion (we were fiercely devoted to the Chicago White Sox) and a pastime (weather permitting, it was a rare day when we did not play it some form or the other).

It was not until we moved north that I became aware of the sport. Shortly after I showed up at Mary A. Todd Elementary, I discovered I was a pariah. The other boys played ball outside during recess. Being completely ignorant of the sport, I was forced to stand on the sidelines and watch with the girls. The shame was palpable, but I had a resource to fall back on. Our father was a lifelong fan (having been taken to games at Comiskey Park by his father and grandfather as a small boy) and readily agreed to teach me the fine points. We went to the sporting goods store, bought a Louisville Slugger "Crackerjack" and a ball, and immediately began lessons in the side yard at 413 Downer Place. By the time second grade came around in the fall of 1952, I was ready to take my place in the playground softball games at school.

I still had a problem I needed to overcome. I did not have a glove and had to play barehanded. That was feasible when playing softball, but it was still a matter of honor to wear a glove of one's own as opposed to having to beg a mitt from someone who was batting—and even by age seven there were athletes who could throw a sharp peg that would sting bare fingers. Once again, Dad stepped into the breach. First, he introduced me to an acquaintance he had made at Our Savior who dealt in wholesale sports equipment. This man would supply me with a genuine Gil Hodges "Trapper" glove for a very reasonable price. Secondly, Dad made sure I got a few extra paid assignments around the house which would allow me to save the required cash (about $4.50) a little faster than if I just saved my allowance (25 cents a week). So before long, I was fully equipped with a bat, ball and glove.

The next phase of my induction into the cult of baseball was a trip to Comiskey Park to see the White Sox in action. Our father and I went by ourselves, Jon being deemed too young for this expedition. I have always believed it was a doubleheader in 1951 and our opponent was the Philadelphia Athletics. In this Internet age, resources are available to permit careful research of such matters and I can't find any games that year that match what I think I remember. 1952 is more of a possibility but the complication is that the most likely home double bill against the Athletics was on a Thursday. Perhaps Dad did take the day off for the game, though that seems unlikely. The exact details will have to remain unclear.

In Chicago, it can often be cold along the lakefront even on warm summer days. Such was the case that day and Dad thought about buying me a jacket, but we were still decades away from the ease of credit cards. He did not feel he could buy me a jacket without getting one to take home to my brother, and he did not have enough money to get two. By late afternoon I was really was freezing, so we departed for the Loop. At Union Station, we rode home on one of the fast trains, the *American Royal*, and because all the seats were reserved for more distant stops than Aurora, there was the great novelty of sitting in the dining car. It had been an exciting day and I was entranced by the proceedings, but disappointed because the Sox lost the first game and we had departed before the conclusion of the second contest.

The suspense over the outcome of the second game was resolved the next morning when our father assured me the Sox had come back to win the nightcap. He introduced me to the wonders of the Chicago *Tribune* sports section and showed me how to read the standings. Best of all, he then turned to the page with the box scores and began my lessons in how to decode and interpret all the wonderful data contained in that mix of columns, rows, and abbreviations. In no time, poring over the sports pages was just about the first thing I did every morning during baseball season. It has been a lifelong habit, though sadly enough, I have long lived in towns not large enough to have a major league team or a publication equal to the *Tribune*. I have also lived long enough to reach an era when the local newspaper has reduced the baseball coverage to less than a half page per day. A website, even if informative, is not quite the equal of holding those pages in your hands while you drink the first cup of coffee or eat your Cheerios.

As he grew up, my brother eagerly joined me in worshipping the game. By the time we moved to 26 South Chestnut he was old enough to play and readily subscribed to the family loyalty to the White Sox. We spent enormous amounts of time playing the game in myriad forms. You could play a game of catch on the sidewalk or a one-on-one game in the backyard, though this put several windows in jeopardy, and our mother did her best to suppress this activity after several accidents. A few years later, someone invented the Whiffle Ball and we could then play safely around the house without concern for property damage. Another favorite game was to toss a rubber ball against the front steps and to try to catch it on the bounce or fly as it ricocheted back to the sidewalk. Naturally, an elaborate point system was devised to score the contest.

By far and away, our favorite games were the happenstance contests that took place at the school playground. On many summer mornings, immediately after breakfast, we'd gather our equipment and set off for the school. There was always someone else there who wanted to play ball and depending on the number of players, we would choose a suitable game. There were never enough participants for a real game, so we had to go to the variations suitable for less than nine to a side. It might be pitcher's hand out, second base over, five hundred, piggy move up, or first bounce or fly. It really did not matter to us in the slightest. Winning the game meant very little, either. What we liked was playing the game— batting the ball, catching it and making a good throw. The thrill of making a good grab or hitting a long one could put a glow in even the gloomiest of days.

In that day, serious organized baseball was a rarity in Aurora. There were only eight Little League teams and few boys played well enough to get accepted. The rest of us played in Boy Scout softball leagues, in games sponsored by the churches and in intramural tourneys at school.   The grade schools organized teams to play softball against each other, but baseball was entirely absent at our junior high and high schools.   It really did not matter much to me anyway, because my enthusiasm far exceeded my gifts for the game. I never learned how to play "hardball" as it was called when played with a regulation baseball and my softball skills were modest at best. I did not have much of an arm and would have been hopelessly befuddled by a fastball pitcher.   My brother, on the other hand, was an athlete and played ball much more gracefully, even as a youngster.   He later played in several different serious amateur baseball leagues, including one in France.

After taking me to my first, our father never again took me to a ballgame.   My first game was the last game he ever went to in his life.   Instead, as my brother got old enough to join the expedition, the task fell upon our mother to take us to see the White Sox.   Nelle was enough of a good sport that she would consent to several outings a summer.   I say good sport because she was not in the least interested in the game.   While Jon and I watched the game, she read a magazine or did a crossword puzzle, entirely oblivious to the proceedings.   When I excitedly told her Minoso or one of our heroes had hit a home run, her response was laconic: "That's nice."   In those days, the clubs did not bar outside food or drink, so we often brought our own picnic.   In addition to baseball, we got Mother's excellent fried chicken.   The only downside was that my brother and I have always been a hex on our team.   When we are in the park the Sox generally lose.

Our fascination with baseball was many faceted.   In addition to the sports page, we regularly followed games on the radio.   On many a summer evening, we drifted off to sleep listening to Commander Bob Elson calling the game on WCFL (AM 1000, the Voice of Labor).   Even after we finally got a TV we still preferred baseball on the radio.   Elson was a careful student of the game, an excellent interviewer and brought an authoritative voice to every play description.   On TV we had to put up with Jack Brickhouse who gabbed endlessly about charities, social events, and celebrities instead of the game.   Not only was he a dunderhead but he made little secret of the fact that the Cubs were his favorites. In 1959, as our Sox were finally making their way to their first pennant in forty years, there was no doubt we would stick with the Commander. We were sitting on the front porch at 26 South Chestnut listening as the Sox clinched the flag with a 4-2 victory over the Indians.

Another important matter involved the acquisition of baseball cards. In those days, Topps was pretty much the only game in town, and there was one choice of packaging. Five cards and a sheet of awful bubble gum (usually stale) were wrapped up in wax paper and cost five cents. It was a lottery with little chance you might manage to find a big star among the many cards you acquired over the summer. We amassed large numbers of duplicates, and efforts to trade with our pals often failed because they had the same cards we did.

The preponderance of mediocre players and unknowns was so high in some years that it was impossible to assemble an All-Star team from the cards you had at the end of the year. Perhaps you might manage to find a few decent pitchers, a catcher and some outfielders, but then the infield would be spotty. Trying to assemble two teams, one for each league was impossible unless you filled in some of the roster spots with real losers. Despite where we lived, we never managed to find many White Sox players and none of our favorites like Fox, Pierce or Minoso.

None of this discouraged our enthusiasm for getting more cards. We scrounged pop bottles, hectored our parents for extra assignments that would be paid, and willingly accepted a pittance for cutting the lawn at several of our neighbors' homes. The meager pay was partially due to the close supervision of Nelle C. Bourgo, who did not want us to be overpaid for work she thought—at least in part—to be an expression of our kindness to others. So, whenever we had managed to assemble some spending money, we would trek down to the Jewel Tea, ever hopeful that the next pack of cards we acquired would have a Willy Mays or a Ted Williams. It never happened and over time, through several moves, our shoeboxes full of those precious cards were pitched out with other household debris, and we are left wondering what fortune was lost by such heedless behavior.

My brother and I were not satisfied with just playing the game and following our team. We also became careful students of the history and lore of the game. Each year we bought the annual *Who's Who in Baseball* and studied all the statistics offered on the 400 or so guys who played Major League Baseball. We memorized batting averages, earned run averages, birthdates, and trades. Every Sunday the weekly year-to-date statistics printed in the *Tribune* were good for at least an hour of detailed perusal. Was this the year Williams would hit .400 again? Was Warren Spahn going to keep up the streak of twenty wins a season? Would Minnie get his usual 100 RBI? These were important matters and we wanted to be informed.

We devoured books on the history of the games containing sketches of the great players and accounts of the most famous games. The question of who was the greatest—Ty Cobb or Babe Ruth—was worthy of very careful consideration. Some events were cheering, such as the many antics of Dizzy Dean, Pepper Martin and the rest of the Gashouse Gang, but we agonized every time we read about Fred Merkle failing to touch second base in 1908 or his teammate Fred Snodgrass dropping that easy fly ball in the 1912 World Series. The gods of baseball were often unkind, and that feeling was reinforced as we learned of the short lives of great people like Lou Gehrig and Christy Matthewson. Still, we thought, what wouldn't we give for just one day in a Major League uniform?

Alas, it never happened, but there has been no chance either one of us could give up our love for the game or our loyalty (no matter how often tested) to the Chicago White Sox. The guests at the wedding reception of Kimberley Bourgo and Chad Baker, held in Plattsburgh, New York, on October 15, 2005, might have noticed some strange goings-on during the festivities. All evening long, two aging fellows kept slipping in and out of the hall together. Closer examination would have revealed the father and the uncle of the bride running out to the parking lot to turn on a car radio so they could keep track of the White Sox playoff game against the Angels. This night the gods were smiling. The Sox won 8-2.

The White Sox

Over their century they have rarely been the best,
but they have always been the team,
first place or last, and since 1951,
through the warm days from April to October,
the first news of the morning
is the box score, the names, and numbers,
either a good or bad start to the day.

The players were the boys who had it all,
who made a living having fun,
who could play the game with a grace
I could only muster in my imagination:
oh, to be a Minoso, Fox or Pierce
moving easily to get the ball,
or stroking a hit that won the game.

Year after year, the Sox finished second,
well behind the Yankees by August,
the hopes of June dying in the heat.
Lonely in their South Side palace,
they were often second in Chicago, too,
never adored like the Cubs,
though most years they played better ball.

All these years, they have been my heroes,
some so briefly they were hardly noticed,
while others could have named an era,
and my pride, once that of a boy
in the prowess of a father or an older brother,
is now closer to a doting grandfather's,
but hope has no age,
and each spring, it might be the year.

Junior High School: Seventh and Eighth Grade

After six years at Mary A. Todd, I was bound for Franklin Junior High, housed in the former high school building and like Todd, conveniently located near our home. It was at most a five-minute walk and I was one of the few students in the school who could go home for lunch, which I sometimes did over the years, though, increasingly I stayed at school and partook of what I thought was excellent fare at 35 cents a meal (including dessert and beverage!).

Junior high offered many novelties. We had lockers and had to learn how to open a combination lock. Our teachers were specialists in just one subject or area (English, science, math or social sciences). Consequently, we had to learn how to find our way around the building to the various rooms where our teachers held forth. It was initially a challenge, trying to make certain you arrived at your next destination in the four minutes allowed between periods. You had to decide whether your path allowed a locker stop to change textbooks, or otherwise live with the burden of extra stuff to haul around. During the first few weeks in September the kinder teachers gave the greenhorns a little slack; the ones made of sterner stuff allowed no quarter and sent the punctually challenged off to the office for a dreaded tardy slip.

Other new and different aspects of school involved the equipment and tools we needed to carry out learning. Lined Big Chief tablets of manila paper were out and replaced by three-ring binders (we especially liked the soft-sided variety that could be zipped closed) and lined filler paper. We added a vinyl pouch with a zipper to carry pencils, pens, a compass, a protractor, and other tools. You could also get rulers with holes punched in them so that they could be secured in the notebook. Section dividers with colored slots were needed to sort out the work we were doing in each subject. In English class, we began the process of learning how to write with pens instead of pencils. We were encouraged to use fountain pens, but ballpoints were allowed, albeit grudgingly by some teachers. The stuffier English teachers required both the pencil draft and the final copy in ink of the weekly essay. Unlike students of today, we did not have backpacks, bags or other luggage, though I do remember one fellow who showed up with an accordion briefcase, and this was thought to be decidedly eccentric.

Seventh grade went smoothly for the most part. I got a preponderance of A's and B's on my report card and sailed through the prescribed course of academic studies: math, English, geography, and general science. English was rather mechanical in its focus. There was little in the way of literature or reading, but a great deal of emphasis on spelling, grammar (diagramming sentences was a major activity), and vocabulary drills. "What does 'tedious' mean? Write a sentence using this word." Geography was surprisingly not limited to the US and Europe as it had been in grade school but included a long examination of South America. We got some homework, but I don't recall it taking a great deal of time on any given evening.

Unlike grade school, the names of some of my teachers have faded with time. Mr. Peterson handled homeroom and geography. Miss Rinehart taught English. I do not recall the names of the math or science teachers. I liked Peterson because he was the first teacher I had who acquainted me with the adult world. He introduced the idea of median incomes, explained the income tax and other economic subjects, and encouraged us to read newspapers and magazines so that we could become good citizens.

The other daily activities—vocational and physical education classes—were not quite so successful. Manual dexterity has never been one of my strengths and I struggled through woodworking, metal shop, mechanical drawing, and printing. It was much the same thing again in eighth grade. That was the end of required shop classes and I was spared any further disgrace in ninth grade. Alas, though, physical education was a trial all three years. Being no athlete, bespectacled and on the short side, I was an easy target for the various bullies. Unlike today, the teachers rarely intervened to protect the victims. The governing assumption was that such behavior was a normal part of school life.

After having flopped at the violin back in third grade or so, I decided to take another whack at instrumental music. The band director was anxious for more members and ran orientation sessions for the new seventh graders, demonstrating several of the instruments. I fell in love with the tenor saxophone and persuaded my skeptical mother to let me try again. This time it all worked reasonably well. The saxophone was a good deal less confusing than a stringed instrument. You memorized which keys to press to get an F sharp or a B natural, and presto, you had it—unlike an unmarked fingerboard where you were never quite sure where to park your fingers. Over time I became a semi-competent member of the ensemble (though no musician) and the band was one of my favorite activities for the rest of my school days.

Eighth grade, in contrast with the previous year, was trying in almost every aspect. After having sailed through seven years of school without much difficulty (or the need to make much of a concerted effort to learn), I ran into some major obstacles and spent much of the year enduring various degrees of anger, confusion, and frustration. It was my misfortune (at least I thought so at the time) to have drawn three relatively obnoxious teachers who only compounded my bad feelings about school. In retrospect, it was not an entirely negative experience. At some point, most of us discover success requires more than going through the motions, and the earlier we learn that, the better. Likewise, sooner or later, we will have unpleasant superiors, and sometimes the only solution is to wait them out.

The first of my tormentors was a math teacher whom I will call Mr. X. There is no way to describe this fellow other than to say that he was a classic bully. He had a knack for finding the easy targets in his class and making them the subjects of his needling. In classic fashion, his victims did not include athletes or attractive girls. At some point he became aware there were still three or four misguided souls in the class who still bit their nails (including me) and decided to make that his crusade. We were informed we had a week to stop our vile habit and that an inspection was looming. If we failed would all be assigned to wear a sign around our necks with "Chomper Brigade" inscribed in large letters.

Naturally, all of us flunked the inspection and were adorned with our scarlet letter, which, he said, had to be worn at all times. Though not much of a rebel, I decided I would not be stuck with this opprobrium throughout the school day and was soon in even deeper difficulties. At this point, I knew I needed to call in the cavalry. We had been raised to believe a teacher was always right, an attitude which our parents strongly encouraged. Thus, despite a certain amount of reluctance, I told our mother the entire tale. As was her style, she was not effusive in her sympathies but took immediate action. The next morning she called the principal and the matter was immediately resolved. Thereafter, Mr. X left me alone, but my continuing apprehension in his presence made it tough for me to concentrate on math.

The next of my three *betes noires* was the science teacher, whom we shall call Mr. Y. He had dozens of rules about how we were to conduct ourselves in class, how we were to prepare our homework, even how we were to conduct our entry and exit from his class. The minute you entered his class you went immediately to your seat with no talking. Exits were to be conducted with similar dispatch and silence. Any hint a student was not paying absolute attention in class was met with a pointed reprimand. Mr. Y was offended by the beltless habits of the "hoods" among us and dictated any boy found without a belt in his class would be immediately sent to the assistant principal's office. In response, we formed a cooperative to help any fellow classmate who might have forgotten his belt and realized he needed one for science class. When the need arose, those of us with a morning class loaned to those in the afternoon sessions and vice versa.

His tests were difficult and he delighted in devising trick questions. He was also obsessed with the idea of preventing any cheating during test taking. Since we sat at lab tables with another student, he dictated that on test days we were to report with all our textbooks and stack them between ourselves. There was to be no eye contact except with the test paper or to the front of the classroom. Hands were never to leave the table. Mr. Y roamed among us continuously looking for any suspicious behavior. He rarely found any hint of infractions because all of us (even the tough kids) were afraid of him. In short, he was overbearing and unpleasant, but at least, unlike Mr. X, entirely predictable.

Lastly, I had to deal with a woman we will refer to as Ms. Z, the English teacher. Ms. Z was in some ways the least and in other ways the worst of my problems. Unlike the other two, she was neither a martinet nor someone who took pleasure in the discomfort of others. She was far more inclined to consider the possibility her 13-year-old charges might have some nearly adult thoughts. Still, she was a ferocious perfectionist, especially in the matter of improving our written communications, and her many quarrels with common errors were to prove a major stumbling block for me, at least through the first half of the year. She was a challenge for anyone who was still trying to learn how to pay attention to all the details, but in the end, I profited from her rigorous and demanding standards.

The major effort in 8th grade English was composition. Ms. Z had a long list of pet peeves, and any paper guilty of one of these infractions was marked with an automatic F. They included confusing *to, too,* and *two*; *your* and *you're*; forgetting the apostrophe in contractions or the possessive, and confusing *it's* and *its*. Since we were assigned an essay every week, those of us who were careless might accumulate a large number of bad grades which would be tough to offset no matter how well we did in the other class exercises. That was certainly my fate and at the end of the quarter, I was looking at a C on my report card.

Along with a C in math, a B in science I was not getting the sort of marks either I or our parents were accustomed to seeing. The only bright spot was American History. Since I was much interested in this subject and had already read a great deal on my own, it was no challenge for me to do well in history. Our teacher was an affable fellow who was more involved in coaching the football team than the classroom, and uninterested in making life difficult for his students. The rest of my report card, though, produced immediate alarms on the home front and an action plan was soon in place.

Dad happened to be around when the offending report card showed up. I got some stern admonitions about putting my nose to the grindstone, but some help and encouragement, too. Dad turned over his second-floor study to me for my homework to ensure I would not be distracted by family activities. A schedule was established which laid out the time to be spent on homework each night and target dates for weekly activities like the dreaded composition, spelling, and so forth. Mother and Dad would check in on me to see how I was doing. They did their best to answer any questions I had and tried to help with anything I found confusing or difficult. Unlike parents of a later generation (myself included) they did not read my work and provide corrections.

All these efforts eventually began to pay off. As the year went by I managed to start avoiding Ms. Z's pitfalls in composition and was even getting an occasional compliment. Getting things done on schedule certainly helped to improve my results and by the year's end, I was doing far better, though my poor start in the first semester left me with only so-so grades for the year. Our father also decided it was high time I upgraded my reading interests and very firmly steered me towards adult reading matter. There is no doubt our parents had certainly helped me to finally figure out how to study effectively, though I can't say I was always diligent in applying my new study skills in later years. As we all know, there is a great divide between what we know and what we choose to do.

The Eighth Grade

Unathletic, short and bespectacled,
I failed in my pursuit of a girl named Susan,
who politely ignored my attentions,
the perfect embodiment of a bad year,
a time of frustration and disaster,
whose exact cause escaped discovery,
whose remediation seemed hopeless.

Deeply distracted by my rejection,
I lost a $10 bill during some trivial errand,
serious money in the Eisenhower era,
for days trying to be suitably remorseful,
though it was good to perceive
that our mother's sermons would only last
until the next need to send me to the store.

School was a trial, the teachers transformed
from the kindly pathfinders of the 7th grade
into hectoring and demanding bullies,
the unholy trio of Mr. X, Mr. Y, and Ms. Z
turning the morning walk into an agony,
replete with worries about the next failure
and what new torture might await.

Unwisely, I sought revenge for some remark,
and received a sound beating,
a good lesson on the strengths of pacifism;
managed an unlikely redemption,
a game-saving catch in a softball tournament,
and time finally crossed into June.
I emptied my locker, collected the yearbook,
and went into the shelter of the summer.

Junior High: Ninth Grade

My final year at junior high was a marked improvement over eighth grade, which stands out as the least successful year in my school career. My grades improved and I began to engage intellectually with some of my studies. I managed to get elected to the student council and continued to enjoy playing in the concert band.

One unfortunate fact of the junior high era was that my brother and I began a long process of separation that continued through my high school and college years. We were never again in the same school together and the growing gulf in our interests and experiences did not really begin to disappear until we both reached adulthood. We did share the summer term at camp for a few more years, but inevitably we spent less and less time together. If we had been only two grades apart rather than four, we might have continued to do more things with each other. This was a distinct change in our lives. Though we both had an assortment of friends, we had been constant playmates through my elementary school years.

Happily enough, I did not have to deal with Mr. X for another year. Ninth grade marked the end of arithmetic and the beginning of serious math with a year of algebra. Unfortunately, algebra and I did not hit it off, and I began to discover a distaste for mathematics which has not served me well in my later years. No doubt, I should have tried harder to conquer this topic, which was never as congenial to me as the humanities. In science, we still had to put up with Mr. Y, but he was a manageable quantity if one were willing to live within his rigid parameters. My favorite teacher was Mrs. Westmoreland, and I had the pleasure of spending two periods a day with her. She taught both English and Latin.

Latin was the only foreign language offered in ninth grade. Though its place in the college preparatory scheme was nearing its end, it was still considered de rigueur for college-bound high school students in 1958. I dutifully signed up and found that foreign languages and I were a good fit. I carefully memorized the vocabulary, studied all the arcane rules of declension, and tried to master all the complexities of tense and conjugation involved in the verbs. It had the attraction of a secret code, which is pretty much the way it was treated. What exactly we were to do with this new knowledge was never entirely apparent, though we were assured it would help us with spelling and vocabulary. It was extremely helpful when I took up French a few years later.

English was my favorite class that year. Charlotte Westmoreland was determined to lead us to appreciate good literature. We studied the five (no more, no less) characteristics of short stories and read some of the classics: Bret Harte, Somerset Maugham (whose story seemed very adult), O. Henry, and Poe. We learned poetry could be written in free verse (though Mrs. W was less enthusiastic about Whitman than Millay or Frost) and worked hard to decode the message in "The Man with the Hoe." *Ivanhoe, Julius Caesar,* and *The Odyssey* all received long and detailed scrutiny, and we began to read adult novels like *A Bell for Adano* for our periodic book reports. Topping the year off, we were assigned the task of writing an autobiography, and my magnum opus (entitled "The Irish Have a Name for It") is still somewhere in one of my files of memorabilia.

Even though we were in the darkest days of the Cold War and amidst all the fretting over the alleged influence of Communism on the nation's young people, there was still little effort (aside from an occasional assembly) to inculcate us with the trappings of patriotism. There were school districts in Illinois with required citizenship training, but ours was not one of them. There was no social studies option of any kind for freshman students. 1958 was in the immediate aftermath of the Sputnik flight and there was a great deal of concern the failings of the American education system might be one of the principal reasons the USSR beat us into outer space. As such, West Aurora District 129 put its emphasis on the core studies of math, science, and English and introduced "advanced" classes.

By comparison with my children's experience in high school a generation later, we had a very narrow and rigid curriculum. Offerings such as psychology, philosophy, and computer science were unknown. On the other hand (unlike later years) a wide range of vocational education was provided for students whose interests lay in those directions. Only four class periods per day were dedicated to academic study. P.E. was a daily requirement and one period was reserved for the band, choir or other electives. Lunch plus the daily homeroom accounted for the rest of the schedule.

After school activities were wide and varied. There were team sports for the athletes, but the rest of us had choices such as crafts, Junior Red Cross, debate, the yearbook, and the school newspaper. I was an enthusiastic member of the model making club and went to Junior Red Cross to please Mother, though I can't recall what we did during Red Cross meetings. Debate was tempting since I was much interested in the news and current happenings, but when I learned it was a sort of elevated parlor game, I dropped out. At 14 I was already a dedicated partisan and the idea of trying to sell something I did not believe struck me as disingenuous.

As we progressed into adolescence, there came the inevitable stirrings, both new and perplexing. For some reason, hard to understand or explain, certain people became objects of great romantic interest. In eighth grade, I had had an utterly unrequited crush on a girl named Susan. Poor Susan! She had done nothing to encourage my mooning and tried to disengage herself from my attention in the hallways at school as politely as possible. Eventually, I got the picture and stopped trying to follow her around. One day near Christmas I tried to muster up enough courage to ring her front doorbell and give her my gift. I walked up and down the block several times talking sternly with my inner self, but to avail. Eventually, our mother got the handkerchief for her birthday.

Our parents (like most I suspect) were in no hurry for me to grow up but tried their best to help me in the social department. During both the seventh and eighth grades I was dispatched off to dancing lessons so that I would not feel unprepared at such events as the periodic sock hops and school dances. As I and the other fellows sadly discovered, though, the stag line was a lonely place to be, since only a few unmatched girls showed up for the casual after-school hops and none at the formal evening events. There were the Friday night dances at the YMCA where girls showed up without dates, but I was not the most courageous of fellows in the matter of asking a girl to dance.

In ninth grade, with much encouragement from the parents, I did manage to invite an old grade school acquaintance named Margaret to the Christmas formal, and we managed to have a nice time. My memory is that Margaret, bless her, even signaled that additional attention would not be spurned. However, I was far from precocious in these matters, and even though I would have been thrilled to have a real girlfriend, I did not have the nerve to push ahead. It was not the last time I would rue the fate of those with faint hearts when it comes to fair maidens.

What Came to Pass (and What Did Not)

The decade of the 1950s was an age of great optimism in predictions of future technological growth. Various and sundry prognosticators projected that driverless cars, cities under the sea, Moon colonies, robotic kitchens and home servants, online education and personal flying cars would be on the scene by the end of the century. Some of these predictions have come true, at least in part. Driverless cars seem possible within the next few decades, though there is considerable disagreement as to how close we are. We do have online education, but its effectiveness is not easily assessed, and both its adherents and detractors are far apart in their conclusions. Robots perform many simple assembly line tasks like assembly, welding, and painting, but robots with the skills to perform a variety of complex tasks are a work in progress. As for the moon, we have been going in reverse. The last moon landing took place in 1972.

Similar predictions in the medical sphere were just as overoptimistic. Life spans of 150, indefinite youth and beauty, the end of all infectious disease, a cure for cancer, an end to famine through synthetic foods, the end of cardiovascular disease and the elimination of the common cold were all predicted. No doubt there has been considerable progress in the treatment of cancer and heart disease. Our father, who died of heart trouble in 1979, was (according to a physician friend of mine) treated by doctors who had few if any effective tools by today's standards. The common cold is still with us and there is little optimism that it will go away ever. New and unanticipated infectious diseases like AIDS, Ebola, and SARS appear on a frequent basis. Pessimistic (or realistic, take your pick) medical researchers suggest that chances for a fully functional and rewarding life diminish greatly after the mid-80s and that reversing this decline may not be possible.

Our life spans have improved by at least a decade, but, ironically, this also leaves us vulnerable to dementia and other debilities, and results in larger numbers of older people requiring costly care at assisted living and nursing facilities. Pharmaceutical research has led to many improvements, particularly in the realm of prevention and management. On the other hand, the cost of such drugs is often staggering and is commonly cited as one of the reasons why healthcare costs in the US so far outstrip those of comparable countries.

An American economist named Robert Gordon recently published *The Rise and Fall of American Growth*. In this book, he argues the changes between 1870 and 1940 were far more substantial than the changes of the next 70 years or so. As he points out, by 1940 or so, many Americans lived in a "modern" setting. They had central heat, electric lighting, flush toilets, kitchen appliances, cars, telephones, and radio. Though we might chafe over the lack of television or the internet in their world, we would not find it entirely alien. Consider how we would react to a life in 1870 which involved fireplaces, outhouses, candles or gaslight, and streets full of horse manure—and that the great advances in public health and sanitation that eliminated such horrors as typhoid, cholera, et cetera, were still in the future.

The most important changes in the recent past have been in information technology and communications. They have had a significant impact, no doubt. However, Gordon argues they are far less significant than the five great changes he identifies for the earlier period: electricity, chemical and pharmaceutical advances, the internal combustion engine, urban sanitation, and modern communications such as the radio and telephone. He argues the reason our recent innovations have paled by comparison is that they are merely different (though yes, better) ways of doing things we were already doing, and not fundamental changes in the way life is lived.

It is not unreasonable to assess the changes of the past sixty years as less than we expected in 1955. We are still heavily dependent on fossil fuels, despite accumulating evidence that our reliance on such energy is having a negative impact on our environment and endangering the future of the planet. We rely even more than ever on our own personal vehicles (though agreed, they are more reliable, safer and more fuel efficient). In the meantime, we have allowed most forms of surface mass transit (save for a few large cities) to go into decline. Air travel, which has increased enormously, has never really lived up to some of its promises. With crowds choking inadequate airports and security requirements, it takes as much total time to travel by air from Chicago to New York as it did in 1936.

The overriding political concern was the outcome of the Cold War with the Soviets. There was considerable discussion of the conflict and the accompanying arms race. The fear of atomic war was palpable, as evinced by the wave of bestselling novels (*Alas Babylon, On the Beach, Earth Abides, Tomorrow*) which dealt with the aftermath of a nuclear attack. There were many movies, magazine articles and TV shows dealing with similar themes. Still, I would not exaggerate the impact it had on daily life. We still went to school, went shopping, and looked forward to the summer vacation. No doubt life was harder for the various Cassandras who fret over such matters more than most of their fellows. But most of us still managed to have fun and spent more time worrying about homework, the bills and the weeds in our gardens than about the Russians or the Chinese.

We could not have imagined the Cold War would come to such an anticlimactic ending—a whimper, not a bang—and I think we would have been tremendously disappointed to learn the aftermath was not an Eden, but pretty much the same drag as before. Somehow the great "peace bonus" never came to be and military spending still eats up about one-fifth of the federal budget. The other "discretionary" portions of the budget have continued to shrink, but not our defense outlays.

We would have also been amazed to learn that the next major enemy would not be a nation-state but loosely organized gangs of religious fanatics out to disrupt civil society with acts of terror. In some ways, Islamic terrorists most closely resemble the anarchists who tossed bombs in the years before WWI. No matter the age, there is always a plethora of reasons for angry young men to commit acts of pointless violence in the name of a higher truth.

Still more things did not change. In 1957, *Why Johnny Can't Read* was a major bestselling book that castigated the educational system for its myriad failures. It suggested the schools were a major national liability, affecting the ability of the US to compete economically and militarily across the globe. In 2016, the same charges continue to be made, and as before, there is utterly no agreement on what needs to be done to "fix" the schools or how to do it. As always, there are lots of accusations, but few concrete plans buttressed with solid data or a willingness to pay the freight.

The American obsession with diet, health food, nutrition fads and so forth was well in place by 1950. It goes back at least to the mid-19th century with the invention of one of the first "health foods"—the beloved cracker introduced by Dr. Graham—and the promotion of vegetarianism by such worthies as Bronson Alcott (the father of a rather successful novelist). The popular magazines of then were full of suggestions for losing weight just as they are today. Then, as now, there were many different and sometimes conflicting strategies being proposed. Unfortunately, current figures on obesity and type II diabetes suggests this may be an area where our progress, in any, has been in reverse

Still, there are many things that are not as we anticipated or were unexpected. Here are a few of those topics in the realm of our day to day culture:

Cohabitation before marriage in the 1950s was largely unheard of save in a few large cities and was thought by most to be utterly unacceptable behavior. In many places, landlords willingly enforced the taboo by demanding proof of marriage from prospective tenants.

Homosexuality was illegal and vigorously prosecuted in most locales. The idea of sanctioning same-sex unions would have been in the moral vicinity of condoning pedophilia.

Many of the social norms of earlier times—such as the formal dress code, prohibitions on sexual display and profanity in movies and

TV, general prohibitions on profanity in public utterances—all have disappeared far more completely and quickly than I would have anticipated.

On a frivolous note, I have observed that celebrity culture has made the leap from grocery store tabloids (which no one admitted to reading in those days) to assume a major role in major media such as network "news" programming, the Internet and the like. It is no longer necessary to apologize for following the various celebrities who are "famous because they are well-known," if I may quote my one-time teacher, Daniel J. Boorstin.

I am sure some will take exception to the suggestion that the revolution in IT is of less importance than some of the great innovations of the past. Agreed, even as late as the 1990s, no one imagined that soon we would be carrying around a device in our pockets that could be a telephone, a camera, a personal computer, an encyclopedia, a dictionary, a calculator, and even, yes—a flashlight. No doubt, the amalgamation of all these functions into one physical form has been most useful. We need fewer things and granted, the new way of doing things may be faster and easier. However, none of this represents any sort of fundamental change in the way we live. We are replacing one way of doing a task with another.

The way these phones are used—for casual communications, watching movies and TV, playing games—is also jarring to me. As an IT guy of the old mainframe school, I grew up in the days when computing was a scarce commodity and carefully allocated only to the most serious and worthy tasks. The thought that there has been such a revolutionary increase in the amount of available computing resource, and that most of it is used for entertainment I do find hard to accept. I agree it's nice to be able to find the closest Italian restaurant with a few clicks, and I am sure that people who live in Boston and New York appreciate being able to search for available parking places on the fly. Still, such applications are not near the top of a list of our society's most serious needs.

There is also much conversation about the way computing is revolutionizing commerce. I am not so sure such developments as Air BnB and Uber are all that revolutionary. They are certainly disrupting the current incumbents in their industries and introducing a new business model, but they are not eliminating those industries quite the way automobiles did in buggy whips and horse breeding. Though I think online shopping is only a new version of catalog shopping in some ways, it is having a major impact on the amount of physical real estate in retail.

I do find a major change in the growth of social media, and I don't mean the ability of people to find their high school classmates on Facebook or telling your 185 Twitter followers you are dining tonight in a Tuscan villa. In the past few elections, the influence of these networks is becoming a significant factor. Politicians do not need NBC, the New York Times or even TV commercials to connect to the public. They can do so with their Twitter accounts or Facebook pages. Increasingly, people are using Facebook, among other sources, to get their news, and it is a fact such outlets are easily used to plant misleading and false information. Whatever one's opinion of the formal news media, one cannot deny that some journalistic standards apply in that world, while they are completely absent in the realm of FB *et al.*

That latter concern has an even broader set of ramifications in publishing as a whole. For some 500 years, we have lived in a printed world of books, magazines, and newspapers. Over time we have developed various and sundry standards and benchmarks that allow us to evaluate the potential veracity and merit of its offerings. Our new Internet world, though, is essentially an inexpensive, enormous and unreliable self-publishing venture. Absent a thoughtful and critical audience, it is a potentially deadly source of misinformation and propaganda.

I will close with two major disappointments, but I will leave the details to people who are more qualified than I to explain why things are as they are. On the economic front, we have seen changes which bode poorly for our future. Back in the fifties, poverty levels were falling and by 1962, we had the most equitable income distribution of any major first world country. By 1997 or so we had fallen to 22nd place, and it has not improved since. Poverty levels have declined since 1960; however, we have leveled out in the 15% range, and the percentage of children living in poverty has increased dramatically.

Secondly, there is the matter of racial and ethnic conflict. Some progress has been made, but it is evident as one follows the news over the past few years that we still have much distrust, prejudice and downright hate at play in our country. The majority white population in 1955 had no inkling it might only be a plurality someday. In 2018, it now understands the demographics of 2040, and the impact on its behavior has not been encouraging. There are days when I think we have made almost no progress in becoming the "One Nation..." of the Pledge. I long ago abandoned the idea we were a melting pot in favor of the salad bowl metaphor, but I will say that back then, I did not expect it would still be such an angry and difficult salad in 2018.

NOTE

I am indebted to the following sources (and to many Google searches) to confirm some of my memories and assertions:

The Rise and Fall of American Growth, book review by Paul Krugman in the *New York Times*, January 31, 2016. (Book Review, page 1)

Neil Irwin, "Tracking Down the True Golden Age of Innovation," *New York Times,* May 15, 2016. (Business Section, page 4)

Epilogue

As I suggested in several places in this tale, life turned out rather well for the Brothers Bourgo.

We both married in our early 20s, are still married to the women we married, and each of us has a son and a daughter. Neither one of was as willing to pursue success quite as relentlessly as our father, but we managed to do reasonably well in our careers and even managed to enjoy what we were doing at least part of the time. At this point, we are both retired and we share a mutual liking for the peace of mind that comes with fishing. Though we only manage to get together a few times a year (he lives in Florida while I am still braving the winter in Pennsylvania), we exchange daily e-mails and we always have a half dozen conversational threads going on.

Other parallels in our lives are worth mentioning. We went to the same high school, and we also spent many summers at a French language school in Maine learning the language last spoken in the family by our great grandfather, Pierre Paul Bourgault. Then both of us attended Knox College in Galesburg, Illinois. He majored in French and I chose history.

After that our paths began to separate. My brother married a woman he had met while an exchange student in France and moved to France for a fifteen-year stay before returning to the United States in 1987. After I spent too many years at the University of Chicago discovering I was not Ph.D. material, I found a job at IBM and stayed with them until I retired in 2003. By turns, Jon was a teacher, an art dealer (he's still dabbling in that), and a manager in a community health center.

Sadly enough, our parents have been gone for many years at this point. Our father had serious issues with hypertension before he was thirty. This led to the heart disease that took him from us in 1979, a few months before his 64th birthday. He was never attentive to his health when younger. Years of overwork, plus all the time he spent living in the rough in the Middle East while managing projects for his engineering firm did not help matters, either.

Our mother was not a poster girl for careful living either, but she managed to live until the age of 78 and died on her birthday in 1983. Her death was a shock to both of us since she had done a masterful job of concealing her declining health in the last year of her life. This was much in keeping with a lifelong practice of never wanting to be the center of attention in her immediate family—while, by contrast, among her brother and sisters, she was always the acknowledged queen bee.

There can be little doubt my brother and I were very much privileged characters in our childhood, and I hope this account has made that very clear. In addition to prosperity, we had all the advantages which accrue from parents who provided love, support, and numerous opportunities to experience a wider world. We profited from a world in which children were accorded more freedom and autonomy, and less in the way of structured activities. There's no substitute for the joy and the duty of finding your own amusements.

One significant thing we did miss was the experience of having grandparents. Since our last surviving grandparent died in 1947, we never got to know any of them except through the memories of our parents and other family members. As one who has had the privilege of interacting with two grandchildren over the past decade, I have learned a great deal about the special relation which can develop between the young and the old. Both sides in the party have a great deal to give and receive, and in my case, I am positive that it has been to benefit of each. I regret Jon and I did not get to enjoy this special relationship as children.

This project arose because Jon and I have both regretted our scarcity of knowledge about our parents' early lives and family backgrounds. With this effort we have assured our progeny will know more about their forebears than we did —perhaps much more than they want to know, but no matter. With this we are on record, and as Casey said, "You could look it up."

It has been a labor of love for the past few years, and though I must take responsibility for the final form and any shortcomings, it has been a joint effort of recollection. Almost every page has a contribution or some memory Jon has furnished to the account, and I am most grateful for his interest and encouragement.

From the beginning always a team!

CPSIA information can be obtained
at www.ICGtesting.com
Printed in the USA
BVHW032116230419
546365BV00001B/51/P